First Steps
to Excellence
in College Teaching

Second edition

By Glenn Ross Johnson

Edited by Bob Magnan

Page layout by James Congdon

Cover design by Darcy Conner

First Steps to Excellence in College Teaching

Library of Congress Cataloging-in-Publication Data

Johnson, Glenn R., 1934-
  First steps to excellence in college teaching / by Glenn Ross Johnson.
      p.   cm.
  Includes bibliographical references (p.).
  ISBN 0-912150-15-7 : $14.25
  1. College teaching—United States. 2. First year teachers—United States. I. Title.
LB2331.J565 1990
378.1'25—dc20   92-17845
                                                                              CIP

Printed in the United States of America.

ISBN 0-912150-15-7

Magna Publications, Inc.
2718 Dryden Drive
Madison WI 53704
(608) 246-3580

Contents

Preface:
By Glenn Ross Johnson 1

1 **Determining Course Objectives:** *Course objectives should explain how students are expected to change as a result of your teaching* 3

2 **Selecting Textbooks:** *Well-organized texts with up-to-date, readable content can be viewed as lectures in print* 7

3 **Those First Class Days:** *Though times of anxiety for teachers and students, the first days of class are crucial for setting the tone for the rest of the semester* 13

4 **Enhancing the Lecture:** *Successful lecturers leave room for and encourage reaction by students* 19

5 **Increasing Student Involvement:** *Discussions, cooperative learning, field studies, critical thinking, and questions all encourage student participation* 25

6 **CIAS — Enhancing Discussions:** *Cognitive Interaction Analysis System helps instructors analyze their verbal interaction with students* 31

7 **Case Studies:** *Using hypothetical situations during lectures lets students attack problems by applying basic concepts and principles learned in class* 43

8 **Term Papers and Oral Reports:** *Formal writing and speaking assignments help students organize their thoughts for others* 49

9 **Testing and Evaluating Students:** *Different types of tests and evaluation procedures have varied advantages and disadvantages* 53

Teaching Creed 65

About the Author 67

Appendix: CIAS Practice Lesson 69

Bibliography 73

Preface

National reports, books by prominent educators, and legislative mandates continue to call for changes in higher education. Students, parents, taxpayers, public officials, governors, and boards of regents are screaming for reform. The more conservative and objective criticisms express a sense of urgency, a plea to systematically analyze the situation within each department and/or college, and to take appropriate action to better prepare beginning instructors and to reward excellent teachers. The bottom line is clear: there is a crisis involving college and university teaching in the United States.

Robert J. Braun, education editor for the *Newark Sunday Star-Ledger*, succinctly summarized the situation in an editorial dated July 19, 1987:

> Ironically, teaching — the art or science of pedagogy — is not even considered a worthy object of study among college faculty. ... College teachers, or at least most of them, do not learn how to teach; they study their discipline and then are afflicted on undergraduates with the assumption that knowledge of subject matter will cover a multitude of sins involving a lack of knowledge about the presentation of that subject matter.
>
> Teaching has never counted for much in higher education or in the careers of those who work in higher education. Students appreciate good teachers, but institutions have not. When college faculty members present themselves for reappointment, promotion, or tenure, what is evaluated are indicators of scholarship, not pedagogy. How extensively a man or woman has published is considered more important than how effectively he or she has taught. The college faculty members who devote their time to improving their instructional presentations have short careers.

Higher education systems have ignored the problem. They need to be proactive in recognizing the importance of teaching. They need to prepare the professors of tomorrow for teaching.

They can do that through programs designed for graduate teaching assistants — the future professors. They can develop programs to support new teachers. They can reward great teachers.

They also need to take corrective action with instructors who display an almost total disregard for students and how they learn. Poor instructors need to be confronted. That should take place at the departmental level. Experienced faculty members need to provide advice and support. The department chair needs to establish formal conferences with beginning instructors and teaching assistants if they need to improve their teaching skills.

Staff members in instructional development centers do not — and should not — have the authority to correct poor teaching situations: determining intervention is not their role. The logical step is for administrators to counsel individuals into seeking the services of personnel in instructional development centers.

Instructional development centers can help new faculty members and teaching assistants improve their instruction — if the teachers are willing to seek help. Instructional development centers are support and service organizations, available to provide knowledge about the art, science, and research of pedagogy. They can lead instructors to water and perhaps make them so thirsty that they drink from the wealth of instructional strategies, but they can't do the teaching for the instructors. Teachers do the teaching, and many do it very, very well.

Because of the widespread attention given to the lack of quality instruction in colleges and universities, I have turned to another way to help beginning instructors and teaching assistants — by writing this book. Faculty members, teaching assistants, and prospective instructors who read the book will find the suggestions tempting. They will build their own knowledge background in pedagogy. They will be able to match their personalities with instructional strategies that might enhance their teaching.

You may want to skim the entire book, then

return to specific chapters at appropriate times. If you are a beginner, you may want to seek advice from experienced instructors who have reputations as outstanding teachers. They can help you with areas in which you may be weak. Once you identify areas where you lack information, you could look at this book's table of contents and decide which chapter to read first, which to read second, and so forth, skipping those areas in which you believe you have real strengths.

It's all up to you now, to take the first steps to excellence in college teaching.

1 Determining Course Objectives

Course objectives should consist of explicit statements about the ways in which students are expected to *change* as a result of your teaching and the course activities. These should include changes in thinking skills, feelings, and actions.

Most instructors tend to state objectives in such broad terms that students have difficulty interpreting them, and instructors would probably have an equally hard time measuring the progress of the students in accomplishing the objectives. Several studies have revealed significant increases in learning when students receive a set of behavioral objectives prior to instruction.

Specificity

Instructors usually need to be more explicit in their descriptions of objectives. How do you write explicit objectives? The key is specificity.

Consider this objective: "The student will know the history of the United States." What is the meaning of the objective? How would you build a course to meet this objective?

The objective is too broad and may be interpreted in many different ways. This lack of clarity and specificity doesn't help you in planning to teach your course. How would you evaluate the success of the students? What types of evaluation tools would you use to determine if the students achieved the objective? The objective simply isn't explicit enough to use.

Consider this objective: "The student will understand the reasons for the Civil War." There would be great disagreement among faculty members if you asked them to measure the success of the students based on this objective.

Objectives should communicate exactly what the instructor wants the students to accomplish. Objectives stated specifically are more useful than general aims. Broad goals and broad objectives may be of value for some programs, but they are not as valuable to instructors when they attempt to plan their courses. Both instructors and students need to know where the course is going.

Instructors might begin to plan their courses with only a few broad statements about concepts, topics, principles, and/or generalizations for the courses. For example, before writing your objectives you might begin with a statement such as the following: "I want these students to know about the important issues that were being debated in the country just prior to the Civil War." From this broad topic, you can move to specific objectives when planning your individual class sessions.

Behavior

Another important point is that the specific objectives need to reflect *student behavior*. If instructors think only about their own behavior, they have nothing that reflects the true progress of the students. The primary reason for objectives written in terms of measurable student behavior is to assess student progress.

How do you write an objective that reflects student behavior? Answer this question: "What do I want students to do at the end of this class period that they probably can't do when they enter my class today?" Having answered your own question, begin to think in behavioral terms that are more easily measurable. You are also beginning to identify what is important for students to know.

Read these objectives:

- "The student will know the names of the Civil War generals."

- "The student will understand the term 'carpetbagger.'"

- "The student will appreciate the concerns of families during the Civil War."

- "The student will enjoy the music of the Civil War era."

- "The student will understand the problems of the South in financing the Civil War."

You must ask if all of the above objectives are important for students to know. Some may be more important than others. For example, history instructors would no doubt agree that understanding the problems of the South in financing the Civil War involves a more sophisticated level of cognition than memorizing the names of the Civil War generals.

Also, since we want to change the behavior of the student, the behavior must be more observable and measurable. None of the above objectives have that level of specificity. How can you measure the behavior of the student at the close of the class session or the end of the course if the objective states that the student will "know" or "understand" or "appreciate" or "enjoy" the situation in the South during the Civil War? One instructor might accept pure recall of information, while others would want evidence of application, analysis, synthesis, or problem-solving.

Clarity of Terminology

Don't use words that are open to many different interpretations. Specific objectives use clear words that make it easier to measure behaviors.

Consider this objective: "During a short essay test, the student will identify the major contribution made by each of three generals for the North during the Civil War, and the student will support the contribution with at least one documented piece of evidence for each."

Note that the last objective is specific and even includes the type of examination to be used.

Sometimes it is advisable to include an acceptable performance level as part of the objective. If only a few students are reaching the minimum acceptable performance level, it is feedback to the teacher that something may be wrong with the instruction. If large numbers of students are reaching a performance level of 90%, it is feedback to the low-scoring students that they have a gap in their learning, they need to study in more depth, or they may need to seek the counsel of the instructor. Acceptable performance levels also provide students with a common reference point to make judgments about their behavior.

For example, consider this objective: "During a regularly scheduled weekly track contest, the student will run the 100-meter dash in less than 11 seconds."

We know the conditions under which the behavior will be performed (during a weekly track contest), the type of measurable behavior (run the 100-meter dash), and the acceptable performance level (less than 11 seconds). This is an example of a specific behavioral objective.

Without the specified acceptable performance level (less than 11 seconds), even I could accomplish an objective to run the 100-meter dash — but I could do it in 30 seconds if there were no acceptable performance level specified.

Selection

Let us return to the Civil War for another type of contrast among objectives. Compare these two objectives:

- "The student will appreciate the problems confronting the South during the Civil War."
- "The student will list 10 generals who fought in the Civil War."

Which of the two objectives is more appropriate for a course in history? The first objective is more appropriate, even though it is not written in specific measurable terms. The second objective is written in specific measurable terms, but it does not require much thinking. This should alert you to the fact that merely stating an objective in specific behavioral terms does not make the objective *valuable*.

Domains

We usually teach to three major domains:

- **Cognitive:** Knowledge and intellectual skills.
- **Affective:** Changes in interests, attitudes, values, appreciations, and adjustments.
- **Psychomotor:** Manipulative and motor skills.

In the preceding section, all of the objectives that referenced the Civil War, except for the one about appreciating the concerns of the families, fall into the *cognitive* domain. The example about the 100-meter dash was a *psychomotor* objective. Of the three types of domains, objectives in the *affective* area seem more difficult to describe in behavioral terms. This is complicated by the lack of valid testing procedures to measure feelings and emotions. Nonetheless, many scholars consider the affective domain to be very important.

One approach to affective objectives is to interact with colleagues to gain their insights. They have been in the business of teaching for many years, and they have watched students march through their programs and enter the world beyond the ivory tower. They have had an opportunity to interact with the employers of their graduates, and have obtained feedback about the behavior of students in the real world. Ask experienced teachers for advice and their reactions to your affective objectives.

Another approach is to refer to a publication by Bloom, Hastings, and Madaus, *Handbook on Formative and Summative Evaluation of Student Learning* (1971), that has some very interesting comments about affective objectives. The authors believe that the cognitive domain is a building block for affective domain objectives.

They believe that the cognitive beginning is the lowest level of an affective hierarchy, since a student is only *aware* of a phenomenon. At the next level, the student is willing to deal with the phenomenon through an expression of *feelings*. Next, the student goes out of the way to *react* to the phenomenon, conceptualizing behaviors and feelings and organizing them into a structure. Finally, students reach the highest level of the affective hierarchy when the structure becomes a part of their life *outlook*.

2   Selecting Textbooks

There are bad texts — which someone else writes — good texts — which we write — and perfect texts — which we plan to write someday.

—Kenneth Eble, *The Craft of Teaching: A Guide to Mastering the Professor's Art* (1976)

Textbooks are common in undergraduate college courses, particularly in required courses. They can be viewed as lectures in print if the textbooks have well-organized chapters, updated content, and are readable. I have listed some additional warnings below.

- **Some textbooks transmit cultural information.** The way the author uses words to describe events and people may be slanted in a positive, negative, or neutral way. The author may have excluded some very important cultural events and minority people when presenting information. If the author's prejudices are apparent, even subtle, you may want to search for a more appropriate textbook.

- **Textbooks reflect the values of the discipline.** There are many different groups within disciplines, and each group may hold some very strong values which may or may not be appropriate for the course you are teaching. The more diverse the opinions and representations of such groups within the textbook, the better.

- **Textbooks promote intellectual development.** How much depth does the textbook reflect? Is the content on a high enough level to challenge the students? Is there evidence of a variety of cognitive levels throughout the textbook and within the questions that the author might raise, e.g., application, analysis, synthesis, problem-solving?

- **Textbooks are capable of communicating specific biases.** This probably sounds similar to the first caution about cultural prejudices. However, in using the term 'bias' I mean 'perspective' or 'orientation.' There may be different theories or ways of approaching the historical signifi-

cance of a happening, and the author may deliberately exclude one or another from among theories and historical events. I lean in the direction of giving fair treatment to competing theories and the treatment of historical events. Eliminating evolution from science books would be another example of bias.

There are other reasons for selecting a textbook carefully. Many students find it difficult to take accurate notes when listening to an hour of uninterrupted lecture. They rely heavily on their textbook to clarify the content as they review their classroom notes. The more closely the textbook corresponds to the students' notes, the more useful it should be to the students.

Most textbooks, unless you've written one for the course, do not always parallel your syllabus. Some instructors create their own textbooks "from scratch" or by compiling the most appropriate materials from various sources. Many others shape their syllabus according to a specific textbook. Most instructors, however, find it necessary to supplement the textbook with ancillary materials. You could distribute readings, copies of charts and graphs, and other handouts, and/or arrange with copy centers or bookstores to prepare and sell supplementary course materials for you.

Two important points: Always obtain permission from the author and publishing company before duplicating copyrighted materials. This is a question of professional ethics, of course, but there are also legal risks that could prove costly. Order textbooks and supplemental materials early so they are available at the beginning of the term; the best textbook in the world is of little value if it arrives too late or the supply of copies is insufficient.

In her article, "Selecting the Textbook," Delivee L. Wright, Director of the Teaching and Learning Center at the University of Nebraska-Lincoln, asks the following basic questions:

- Will you supplement the content in the textbook? Or will the textbook be used to supplement what you state in the classroom?

- Do you want the textbook to be the main focus of the course? Or is it merely one of several sources you want students to use?

Cost

Textbooks cost more than ever, and this makes the price of a text an important consideration. Eble, *The Craft of Teaching: A Guide to Mastering the Professor's Art* (1976), summarizes the problem: "For most courses, there never has been such an abundance of useful text materials. Faculty members who tend to take advantage of these riches may total the costs for an individual course, but fail to consider that students are expected to buy books for four or five courses."

High costs may discourage some students from purchasing and using all of the textbooks selected for a single course. Faculty must take special care in selecting the number of books they will require students to buy, eliminating those rarely referenced during lectures or on examinations.

You may want to consider putting the less-important readings on library reserve. If you do so, visit the library and verify that the readings are actually on reserve. Don't assume anything — or expect students to tell you if a reading is unavailable.

Using the Textbook

Instructors should learn to use a textbook without repeating what is in print. For example, part of a class period might be used to clarify or supplement the material in the textbook, while the remainder of the time could be devoted to discussions or to asking questions involving application, analysis, synthesis, or problem-solving based on the material presented in the textbook. As Eble (1976) points out, "If ... stimulating learning through interaction between student and teacher is the chief aim, then what the teacher does in class differs in kind and substance from what the text does."

Instructors who merely repeat the text are wasting valuable opportunities for real teaching activities, encouraging students not to read, boring students who've prepared, and/or undermining attendance, participation, enthusiasm — and learning.

Brown and Thornton, *College Teaching: A Systematic Approach* (1971), suggest that the instructor supplement, elaborate, interpret, or clarify ideas that appear in the textbook.

Instructors can help students learn how to use the textbook as a study guide by discussing its organization and treatment of topics, by suggesting ways to study it systematically, and by emphasizing the review, graphic, and index materials.

For example, the instructor could become a role model for students by simulating how he/she read the first chapter, pointing out that one usually begins with an overview of the chapter by reading the title, by analyzing the opening paragraph and the summary paragraph in the chapter, and by raising questions that were triggered by the overview. The instructor could also contact the publisher to find out if there is an instructor's guide for the book and to ask if there are special materials, such as graphs, charts, maps, etc., that are available from the publisher.

Why Use or Not Use a Textbook?

Fuhrmann and Grasha, *A Practical Handbook for College Teachers* (1983), and Brown and Thornton (1971) provide excellent guidelines for answering this basic question, in terms of advantages and disadvantages.

Advantages:

- Textbooks provide students with uniform bodies of basic information.

- Textbooks contain an organized, sequential approach to the study of a subject, in a simple style, and at an appropriate reading level.

- Textbooks include pertinent illustrations, graphs, maps, and diagrams.

- Textbooks present a large amount of information efficiently.

- Textbooks are organized in such a way that you could develop the course syllabus in sequence with the chapters in the book.

- Textbooks contribute to motivation if the expert's insights are presented in an exciting and challenging way.

- Textbooks provide opportunities for students to reason and expand their understanding if the author has inserted key questions throughout the text.

- Textbooks reduce the in-class time needed for integrating content, allowing for application, analysis, and problem-solving.

Disadvantages:

- Textbooks become outdated and do not provide current innovations.

- Instructors may rely on textbooks as the only source for content, instead of using the information in the book to build concepts, illustrations, examples, and theories within the context of their students' background.

- It takes time to select good textbooks.

- Textbooks may become a crutch for writing objectives. Select textbooks according to your objectives; don't let textbooks determine your objectives.

- Textbooks allow little or no room to select content from more original sources and current research reports.

A Systematic Checklist for Selecting Textbooks

In "Selecting the Textbook," Wright (1987) offers an excellent checklist as a systematic guide for selecting textbooks. I present this checklist here, with some minor modifications. You may want to reference this checklist the next time you select your textbooks.

Title:

_____

Author(s):

_____

Publisher and publication date:

_____

Use the following scale to assess each criterion:
1 = very adequate;
2 = adequate;
3 = neither adequate nor inadequate;
4 = inadequate;
5 = very inadequate.

Scale	Criterion
1 2 3 4 5	**Bibliography:** Are the citations current and appropriate?
1 2 3 4 5	**Author(s):** Are they recognized as knowledgeable in the field in which they are writing?
1 2 3 4 5	**Reviews:** Have professional journal reviews been good?
1 2 3 4 5	**Topic emphasis:** Do topics correspond to objectives for your course?
1 2 3 4 5	**Sequence:** Are topics arranged in a desirable sequence? Can they be adapted without disrupting the usefulness of the book?
1 2 3 4 5	**Content:** Is it accurate? Is the point of view consistent with the current thinking in the field? Are recent developments included?
1 2 3 4 5	**Bias:** Is it free of nationalistic, racial, or sexual bias?
1 2 3 4 5	**Concepts, Principles, Generalizations:** Are they clearly developed? Can you read basic facts and information in the book and find that they lead you to concepts, principles, and generalizations?
1 2 3 4 5	**Details:** Is detail sufficient?
1 2 3 4 5	**Explanations:** Are they clear and Succinct?
1 2 3 4 5	**Reading Level:** Is the readability level of the text appropriate for the average student enrolling in your course?
1 2 3 4 5	**Presumed Student Experience:** Do students have a sufficient background to understand the author's material?
1 2 3 4 5	**Titles, Headings, Subheadings:** Do these help the student visualize the organization and relationship of content?
1 2 3 4 5	**Summaries, Review Questions:** Are there study aids? Do they help students generalize, apply, evaluate content, simulate critical thinking, or require problem-solving? For example, after the author presents some important information, does he/she challenge readers with a simulated happening or a real problem to solve?
1 2 3 4 5	**Table of Contents, Preface, Index, Appendices:** Are these adequate and useful? For example, does the author provide a succinct outline of the book in the table of contents? Does the author give a good overview in the preface regarding where the book is going and the type of audience he/she is addressing? Is the index complete with key words and important

terms? Do the appendices include any important survey instruments or measurement devices that were referenced in the body of the text?

1 2 3 4 5   **Sources:** Are these documented adequately?

1 2 3 4 5   **Illustrations:** Are these accurate, purposeful, properly captioned, and placed near the related text?

1 2 3 4 5   **Graphs, Tables, Maps, Charts:** Are these clear, pertinent, and carefully done?

1 2 3 4 5   **Durability:** Is the book constructed well? Is the binding flexible?

1 2 3 4 5   **Type:** Is it clear, easily readable, and large enough?

1 2 3 4 5   **Format:** Do page size, column arrangement, margins, and white spaces contribute to communicating ideas? Do they allow for supplemental note-taking? Does the format invite reading or impede the reader?

1 2 3 4 5   **Price:** Is the price reasonable for the extent to which you will use the text for assignments?

1 2 3 4 5   **Size and Weight:** Will the text be easily carried to class? Remember, students may have to carry several materials for many classes, sometimes considerable distances.

1 2 3 4 5   **Instructor's Manual:** Are supplemental materials, teaching aids, test questions, and suggested strategies included?

1 2 3 4 5   **Supplemental Workbook, Computer Software:** Are resource materials suitable for some or all students to purchase?

1 2 3 4 5   **Measurements for Student Achievement:** Are test items or other devices for assessment provided?

Developing a Syllabus

The course syllabus should reflect the overall direction of the course and the objectives you have in mind for the students. Colleagues can show you how they taught the course during previous semesters. Most content decisions are up to you, unless there is a required departmental syllabus.

Distribute the syllabus, provide time for students to read through it and invite students to ask questions about items in it. There are several items to incorporate in the syllabus.

On the first page you should have your full name, title, office location, office phone number, and office hours. You would be surprised at the number of students who are reluctant to ask questions about these items. Draw a diagram on the blackboard so they can better understand the location of your office. Tell them that you adhere to your office hours, and encourage them to take advantage of those hours if they are having problems. Some instructors include their home phone numbers, while others prefer privacy when at home and away from the campus.

Include the title of the course, catalog number, semester hours of credit, course meeting location, time and days when the course meets. These may seem like mundane items, but many students attending college for the first time get confused about such items. Some even attend the wrong course or wrong section of the course for an entire session before they realize their mistake. Include the above in the syllabus and help save some students from such embarrassment.

Include a short course description and list any prerequisites. Be sure they coincide with the statements in the catalog. You don't want to find yourself on the carpet with administrators because you decided to arbitrarily change such items — the descriptions and prerequisites probably reflect numerous hours of deliberation by your colleagues. The students have no excuse if later they claim, "I didn't know the course was going to cover that kind of stuff" and "I don't have the background information."

Include the titles of basic texts by authors and specify which editions you will be using. Bookstores have big sales of used books, and many students sell their copies at the close of a course. A problem emerges if new students purchase earlier editions that no longer provide current information. Sometimes in literature courses there are problems with various editions of the same work, since they have different critical apparatuses and pagination, making assignments and class references confusing.

Include a set of general objectives for the course; don't include your daily lesson objectives. I have found that four or five important objectives serve a vital purpose in guiding the students. Review the earlier section on objectives before you write these for your syllabus.

List a set of topics and activities for the

semester. Include any special dates for examinations, lab exercises, and due dates for papers. These are very helpful to beginning students and also help keep you on track for the semester.

You should also list the bibliography, library reserve room references, and audio-visual materials with their locations. Don't be surprised if one of your students asks, "What's a reserve room?" Give the student a polite answer; even tell him where it is located in the library and what restrictions apply when using reserve materials. Be prepared to outline procedures for using materials on reserve. Sometimes students who are unfamiliar with "routine matters" may avoid crucial preparation or supplemental work.

Include a statement about academic dishonesty, taken from your institution's student handbook to ensure there are no misunderstandings. Take time during the first class session to explain plagiarism if you are requiring written work. Discuss some examples of plagiarism.

There are some additional items you may want to consider including in the syllabus; it depends on you and the course you are teaching:

- What is your stand on absences? Does your institution have a policy on absences?
- Will you allow a make-up if a student misses an exam? How will you deal with late term papers?
- Do you want to describe your criteria for grading term papers? How will grades be determined?
- Does the institution have a policy on grading? For example, are you *required* to use a standard curve when grading? What will constitute an A, B, C, D, or F in the course?

Final Details

Make arrangements for teaching aids well before the first class meeting. Check the overhead projector, microphone, film projector, or slide projector; ask a technician to show you how to replace bulbs and/or batteries. Find out where you can obtain immediate assistance if the equipment malfunctions. Many an excellent lesson plan falls apart because of equipment problems.

Stand in the spot where you will lecture. Practice with the equipment you'll be using during class. Note how well your voice carries and how your handwriting looks on the blackboard or on the projection screen. Have another person sit in various seats to give you feedback from students' perspectives.

3   Those First Class Days

How important is that first day of class? Crucial! Both students and instructors find that first session anxiety-producing. But the first day and those that follow can also be exciting if properly handled. Here are a few ideas to make the first class session a good beginning for an excellent semester.

Introduce yourself to the students, then have the students introduce themselves. Have them mention their fields of study, hometowns, campus residences, hobbies, and families. This "ice-breaker" reflects your interest in the students. It also makes it easier for students to form relationships early in the semester, so they can work together, both in and outside of class.

Ask students to identify some problems or issues they hope will be covered during the course. Build a list of such items on the blackboard. Ask questions that will clarify exactly what the students are seeking. These short interactions also help to build an accepting climate within the classroom. The students begin to realize that you are not the ogre they may have anticipated.

Take attendance, for at least the first few meetings. Many instructors overlook this dreaded burden, but it can express your interest in the students as individuals, with faces and names. It also implies that attending class is important.

Distribute the course syllabus and highlight the more important items. Discuss the purpose of the course and your requirements. Review important dates and compare them with the institution's calendar of events: the deadline for course withdrawals without penalty, the date when grades are due, religious holidays, and so forth. Review institution and department regulations and look for information about giving exams on religious holidays, giving makeup tests, and providing information to students about the appeals process. Tell the students your expectations about student collaboration on homework, work turned in late, grading, and successful strategies for studying for your course.

Students may react to your behavior by imitating you, and they may use your procedures when they interact with others. If you use negative, aggressive behavior and sarcastic remarks with students during the first class session, it is possible that the students will mimic such behavior.

A high-anxiety student seems to perform poorly on a task if he is reprimanded throughout a performance. This can be explained as conditioning (see classic studies by B.F. Skinner, Ivan P. Pavlov, John Watson, and Edward Thorndike as reported by Wittrock in *Learning and Instruction*, 1977). The student may be conditioned to feel uncomfortable in similar classrooms during future courses because the sarcastic professor becomes the student's "conditioned stimulus" creating high anxiety and poor work.

In contrast to the above, I believe you should be curious, considerate, kind, imaginative, and flexible, thus providing a more enriching model for students to copy.

Some instructors erroneously assume students are lazy. Students may be highly motivated to learn if the subject is of value to them, but they may be bored to tears if the instructor uses the same illustrations and examples as the textbook. The professor should provide examples which are different from those in the text.

Instructors can fall victim to another trap if they believe students are stupid. Less-talented students may start the course with high expectations, but may be turned off because the instructor uses illustrations they don't understand. Meanwhile, instructors may believe they're making the course challenging. Use relevant illustrations appropriate for the experiential background of students so their attention spans improve.

Some instructors like to conclude the first class session with an assigned reading. Others require something in writing, to be collected during the next class session. The idea is to communicate to the students from the very beginning that the course is *important*. Therefore, whatever the assignment might be, make sure it is *valuable*, not just a "Mickey Mouse" activity.

Review any safety rules and regulations if a lab or a field experience is involved. You may want to demonstrate some precautions students should take throughout the course. If the class is taught in the evening, you may provide some additional cautions about campus security.

Some instructors give students a few sample test items or examples of quality term papers from previous semesters. Give the students some hints about how to study for your exams. Some instructors also develop and administer a "diagnostic" evaluation the first day of class. These "diagnostics" are not assigned grades; they cover prerequisite knowledge or skills needed to succeed in the course. After checking the responses and analyzing the data, you may want to reorganize the tentative schedule if students already have mastered the information for one or more topics. Sometimes the data indicate a need for a review of prerequisites prior to undertaking a topic. You may even have students who are totally lacking in the prerequisite knowledge or skills, and you may have to counsel them out of your course and into a course where the prerequisites are covered.

Beyond the First Few Days

Greet the students individually as they enter the room each day. This helps establish rapport, and it provides them another opportunity to comment about the progress of the course.

Start and finish your class on time. If you start on time, the students know that you mean business, and they will make a more concerted effort to get there for the beginning of the class session. Close on time because some students will have other courses to attend, sometimes on the other side of the campus.

After you get better acquainted with the students, set up a three-member advisory committee to meet with you each week in your office and provide feedback. How are the other students progressing in the course? Are there any problems so far? What have the students found as strengths?

Ask the students if they want to form study groups and support groups. Have them meet and develop a group roster with addresses and telephone numbers, if they don't consider such to be an invasion of privacy.

Relax! Use humor if appropriate. Project a cartoon on the screen, relate the cartoon to the day's content. Students will look forward to seeing the cartoons when they enter the classroom. Tell a story about yourself, one that shows the human side — a "goof" that you made,

something you forgot to do, a special event like a wedding anniversary. Some instructors play music while the students enter the room. When the music stops, it cues the students that the class is about to begin.

During class move around the room — without becoming a distraction. This gets you closer to the students, particularly when a section is in an auditorium. It is also surprising how your closeness to students stops them from dozing during class time.

Share something from the *Wall Street Journal*, the *New York Times*, or a prominent city newspaper, or tell them an anecdote during the first few minutes. This provides time for the students to settle in for the day's lesson.

At the close of the class session, congratulate the student who asked the best question during the period, and ask the others why the question was the best.

Use relevant illustrations and examples. Try to relate the content to the geographic and cultural setting of the institution. These examples should be appropriate for the content you are presenting, and they should be beneficial in reaching the purpose of the lesson. Consider using examples that will provide images in the minds of the students, ones they can almost feel, smell, and taste.

When you require homework, collect it and provide feedback in writing as soon as possible. The students put a lot of time into their homework — they want to know that you have enough respect for them to read their work and to provide feedback.

Provide an "advance organizer" for the beginning of your presentation, e.g., "Today, we will discuss exponential functions." Advance organizers are broad, goal-oriented statements or assignments that help students establish a general mind set for what is about to happen during a lesson. A short reading assignment about the topic, but lacking specifics, would be considered acceptable as an advance organizer.

Encourage the students to interact with you. Ask questions, then pause long enough for the students to organize a response. Acknowledge questions immediately. Many students must muster up the fortitude to raise their hands and ask questions — strike while the iron is hot.

Praise students when they give appropriate answers: "That's a great response" or "That answer is particularly important because ...." Be specific in your praise: be sure you know why the response is good. If a student gives an incorrect response, turn to another student and ask if he/she agrees and why. The student giving the incorrect response is less likely to feel embarrassed than if you simply say that he/she is wrong.

All of the above suggestions set the climate for the entire semester. Do the right things so you don't look bad. The journey begins with a single step. Take that first step carefully, and the long journey through the semester will be much easier and more productive.

Deciding on Strategies

The following five major interacting variables within the classroom will determine to a great extent how successful your lessons will be:

- All of the characteristics associated with the instructor, e.g., personality, knowledge, skills, experiences.

- All of the characteristics associated with the students, e.g., prerequisite knowledge and skills, personality, attitude toward the subject under study.

- The structure of the knowledge, e.g., linear or non-linear.

- The classroom setting, e.g., movable chairs and tables versus fastened-down furniture; small class size versus one that is over-flowing with students.

- The instructional strategies you select.

Instructors should vary their teaching strategies to suit the objectives established for the lessons. One instructor might use a case study or simulation one day while another uses discussion. How do teachers determine which strategies to use?

Remember the section in this book on objectives. Ask, "What do I want the students to be able to do at the end of today's lesson that they probably can't do before the lesson?" Then, once you've identified the daily objectives, ask, "Which instructional strategies will probably be best in helping the students reach my objectives for today's lesson?"

- If your objectives include a lot of factual information, lectures may be quite appropriate.

- If your objectives include affective behavior (values, attitudes), role-playing and simulation may be more effective than lecturing.

- If your objectives involve the manipulation

of science equipment (psychomotor skills), provide opportunities for students to use the equipment. A lecture would again be inappropriate, although a very short introductory and motivating mini-lecture might be essential, e.g., a type of "Don't blow us up today by mixing the wrong chemicals" introduction to using the equipment as you demonstrate the correct procedures.

- If your objectives involve group dynamics, you would want to consider experiences that call for group activities.

- If your objectives include a review of previous content, you might want to use a strategy where you ask questions about the subject and the students have to respond to those questions.

Your personality and learning style will be influential in helping you decide which approach to use for the various objectives. Galbraith and Sanders, "Relationship Between Perceived Learning Style and Teaching Style of Junior College Educators" (1987), reported a very high correlation between preferred learning styles of instructors and their preferred instructional methods. In other words, most instructors tend to teach their courses as they would take them: the teacher thinks as a student. This is certainly normal — but be aware of how and how much our learning determines our teaching.

Ask another faculty member or a departmental student advisor about the level of preparation and ability expected of students in the course. Note which curricula are heavily represented in your class. This information, available on class rosters, may point to prior student preparation in your area. It can help you in selecting examples and making assignments that relate to students' experiences.

When communicating basic facts, the lecture approach is the more standard strategy at the postsecondary level. However, there are a number of very different strategies you should begin to add to your repertoire. (I will discuss several of the strategies during the next few chapters.)

Assume that you have listed your objectives and identified a number of different strategies that could be used to accomplish the objectives. What do you do next? Based on knowledge you have about your students and how they might best learn the content associated with the objectives, select those strategies that appear to be better for the majority of your students (see MSLQ below). Also, consider any economic factors by answering the following question: "How much money will be required for the strategy (buying audiotapes, developing 2" x 2" color slides, printing or buying a simulation program, renting a movie) and how much time (also an economic factor) will be required to prepare the lesson?" Answer another question: "Do I need additional space, microcomputers, study carrels, staff, and materials to make the delivery system work?"

If I had to select one guideline that supersedes all others, I would have to choose *learning*: how students learn must be the central focus when selecting a strategy. We are teaching so students learn. As obvious as this assumption might seem to me, it is not embraced by many teachers: I just tell the students the facts; it's up to them to learn, as if *telling* and *teaching* were synonymous.

Using the MSLQ to Determine Strategies

A group of researchers associated with the National Center for Research to Improve Postsecondary Teaching and Learning (NCRIPTAL) developed a diagnostic tool to assess the learning styles of students (Pintrich, McKeachie, Smith, Doljanac, Lin, Naveh-Benjamin, Crooks, and Karabenick, *Motivated Strategies for Learning Questionnaire [MSLQ]*, 1988). The instrument was designed to gain insight into student motivation for learning. Another NCRIPTAL group developed a set of teaching tips that overlay the MSLQ (Johnson, Eison, Abbot, Meiss, Moran, Morgan, Pasternack, and Zaremba, 1991). A new manual for the most recent version of the MSLQ has been published by NCRIPTAL (Pintrich, Smith, Garcia, and McKeachie, 1991).

I believe instructors can administer the MSLQ in their classrooms, using computer-scoring answer sheets, and obtain a good snapshot of where the students fall among the 21 categories of the instrument. This diagnostic approach might help instructors select from a potpourri of instructional strategies appropriate to the course and lesson objectives and the basic motivational needs of the bulk of the students enrolled in the course. How?

The next several pages provide examples of how you could use several of the MSLQ categories to help you with instructional strategies for various lessons. Most of the suggestions, as indicated in parentheses, come from Cross and Angelo (1988), *Classroom Assessment Tech-*

niques: A Handbook for Faculty. The titles they used to describe the examples are listed in the parentheses at the end of each suggestion.

Rehearsal Strategies

Here is an instructional example, detailed by Cross and Angelo, that might help students who are weak in this area. You could have the students list information they believe other students should know to be successful on a forthcoming examination. Why? The students are actively involved, and their statements can serve as feedback to the instructor, who can determine how much information the students can recall. Ask the students to share their information during group sessions. Develop a set of topics and distribute the list to the students to review, either in groups or alone, if gaps in knowledge are apparent ("Focused Listing").

Elaboration Strategies

You could tell students to paraphrase the material covered in a lecture or assigned reading. Why? Students will better understand how well they have grasped the more important elements in a lecture or assigned reading if the instructor collects their summaries and provides them with feedback ("Directed Paraphrasing").

You could engage the students in a structured written assignment. Why? The activity gets students actively involved as they clarify their analytic and writing skills. Divide the class into two groups, and assign each group a different problem. Have one group of students role play executives, managers, or political analysts who scrutinize the memos written by the other group of students. The instructor should identify the role of the student, the audience for the memo, deadline for completion of the memo, and length of the memo (usually two or three pages). The instructor should probably write a memo for each assignment and then compare elements included in his/her memo with those of the students. After reading the students' memos, the instructor can provide feedback to the students ("Analytic Memos").

Metacognition Strategies

You could have students describe the steps they used in solving a problem. Why? This activity forces students to think about the information processing they have used to reach a conclusion. After demonstrating your own problem-solving process, you can provide a situation that would be new to the students and then direct them to write down the steps they used to solve the problem ("Documented Problem-Set Solutions").

You could provide a written assignment that requires the students to use critical reading skills. Why? Students must develop critical reading skills to assist them in analyzing what they read. Students could be required to outline a chapter in the textbook or the content in a handbook. You can then review their outlines to see if they can identify the important elements in the material while they are paraphrasing. It would be helpful if you would provide feedback to students about their critical reading skills ("Do & Say [Function & Content] Analysis").

Organization Strategies

You could have students categorize a set of items drawn from class lectures and/or assigned readings. Why? Students become actively involved with a process that helps them store information for retrieval at a later date. Provide a list of important items and ask students to place them inside a matrix that has a set of labels for various categories. For example, a set of terms could be listed along the left side of a matrix, category labels could appear across the top of the matrix, and the students could place a check mark at the interaction of a term with the proper category label ("The Defining Feature Matrix").

Another organization strategy would be to engage students in creatively summarizing a topic. Why? Students need to learn techniques that will help them summarize information into smaller units so they can better recall the information at a later date. Cross and Angelo have presented a structure for such summarizing, which they claim can be used to summarize almost everything that is represented in the declarative form. Students first complete a matrix where the left column is labeled "Question" and right column is labeled "Response." The students respond to the following questions (WDWWHWWW): Who? Do What? To What or Whom? How? When? Where? Why? After completing the matrix, the students must use the data in the response column to summarize in sentence form (One-Sentence Summaries — "WDWWHWWW").

Intrinsic Goal Orientation

You could attempt to identify the learning goals of the students. Why? You can identify how closely the learning goals of the students correspond to the learning goals for the course. The instructor could tell the students to reference the instructional goals in the course syllabus and rank order the list in line with their personal perceptions of the importance of each goal. This activity requires each student to assess his/her personal learning goals with your course-specific instructional goals ("Student Goals Ranking").

You could ask the students to determine how successful they think they will be in your course. Why? Students will better understand what they need to do to complete the course. The instructor could provide a checklist of topics covered in the course and the skills needed to successfully complete the course; students would indicate how well prepared they were to master the checklist of topics and which skills they thought they lacked ("Course-Related Interest and Skills Checklists").

Help-Seeking Behavior

If the students and you have access to computerized electronic mail services, use the system to write an open letter to the students, encouraging them to respond, and keeping their responses personal and anonymous. Why? This is one of the more non-threatening ways for students to express frustrations that you may or may not realize exist. Include a few questions about your instruction or a difficult session or topic that the students may have encountered during the course. Analyze the students' responses and follow up with appropriate actions and comments ("Student-Teacher Electronic Mail Messages").

Does making learning the central purpose of your teaching make for more work? You bet it does! You must rethink the various theories and models of learning for clues about how best to present material to your students:

- Do you want to emphasize discovery?
- Do you want to stress operation processes?
- Do you have a behaviorist view that emphasizes stimulus-response theory?
- Do you support human modeling that stresses vicarious reinforcement?
- Do you need to administer a learning

questionnaire to a typical group of students who will be taking your course so you can find out more about their learning styles?

You may find the above questions overwhelming at this time in your career, however, I believe you should begin to give such questions more of your time. You are *beginning* your teaching career — you have many years ahead to delve into the above in more depth.

The following are examples of other strategies one could use with the MSLQ. These are taken from *Teaching Tips for Users of the Motivated Strategies for Learning Questionnaire* (Johnson et al., 1991).

Task Value

Increase personal contact with your students by scheduling 15-minute office conferences so you can discover more about the students, their interests, their goals, and their needs.

You could have the students complete an inventory in which they identify topics of most interest, topics of least interests, and topics that are not covered in the textbook but which they would be interested in pursuing.

After you get to know your students, you can have them read current events that relate to what they are studying in your courses. Students could share those during class time or you could post the articles and cartoons on a bulletin board.

Vary your strategies by inviting guest speakers to address the class or by having panel discussions.

Critical Thinking

Divide the students into groups. Have each group pursue a different problem situation. Next, have students "role-play" people who might become involved in the problem situations — Chief Executive Officer, Business Manager, members of different ethnic groups — while each group makes a presentation about its proposed solution to the assigned problem.

Another critical thinking strategy is to give your students an assignment to read prior to the next class session. During that next session, ask them probing questions that require critical thinking. Finally, serve as a model and demonstrate the way that you analyzed and critiqued the written assignment; tell them about data collected, conflicting viewpoints, hypotheses to be tested, etc.

Another good critical thinking exercise requires the students to create dialogues involving great people in history. Give the students the dates, settings, and names of the historical persons, then "role-play" specific scenarios, e.g., U.S. Grant meeting with his staff prior to engaging in a battle with Robert E. Lee.

Time and Study Management

Have your students design a wall calendar with blocks for every day of the month. Require the students to fill in the blocks with reminders of when papers are due, dates of exams, etc. Then tell them to estimate reasonable amounts of time they should be devoting to each of the items listed on the wall calendar.

Have the students form groups in which they will explore distractions that impede their progress in completing assignments, preparing for exams, etc. This type of "peer-group discussion" will help your students reduce anxiety while learning how their peers cope with distractions.

Teaching Tips for Users of the Motivated Strategies for Learning Questionnaire provides additional illustrations and examples of learning strategies to use in conjunction with the MSLQ.

4   Enhancing the Lecture

Since instructors continue to select the lecture more than any other instructional strategy, I think we should begin with techniques that will enhance your style of lecturing. Clarke, "Building a Lecture That Really Works" (1987), suggests that "successful lecturers often succeed because they leave room for students to react, encourage reaction, and scan the audience for clues about the health of the interaction. They know the reaction to look for and take steps to ensure that reaction" (p. 54).

But how do we leave room for reactions? How do we encourage students? What clues can serve to guide us? And how do we ensure proper reactions from our students? We all know the following advantages of the lecture approach:

- We believe it is time-efficient.

- We can reuse the lecture in different sections of the same course, and we can repeat the lecture from semester to semester.

- We feel comfortable because we *know* the *content* has been *presented.*

- We can provide organization, particularly if the structure of the knowledge is linear.

- We can highlight major facts, concepts, principles, and generalizations that students might overlook in their reading.

McLeish, "The Lecture Method" (1976), justifies the use of the lecture by discussing five reasons for using the strategy:

- Students are too immature or unresponsive to learn via self-directed reading on their own.

- The instructor can go over the material in a textbook, using different words and illustrations to clarify concepts and understandings.

- Complex scientific information that hasn't been published in textbooks can be introduced.

- The professor can be the critic of the material in the textbook.

- We can reach large numbers of students.

Lectures also have limitations. Instructors may simply read the materials or present the information in a boring manner or with a monotonous voice. The lecture format may prevent students from becoming actively involved for the entire class session. How can we overcome such limitations of the lecture?

Be Knowledgeable

Remain knowledgeable about the content you are teaching. Attend seminars and conferences where others are presenting similar content. Take notes during their presentations, paying particular attention to new ideas and new research information.

Read the journals for your discipline, and ask publishing companies for review copies of new textbooks. Develop a scheme for taking down important information presented in the journals and textbooks. If someone has a particularly good schematic drawing or graph, write to the author and the journal or textbook publisher and ask for permission to make a transparency copy of the page to use in your class. Be aware of copyright laws since you should only use this approach on a limited basis. If you ask, most publishers will send you a summary of the copyright laws or direct you to a source.

Store your notes and related materials; develop an appropriate file system so you can easily retrieve such items when you need them for classes or for revising your course. Reviewing and revising your lectures is another way to remain knowledgeable; students joke about instructors who bring to class their yellowed sheets of lecture notes that have coffee stains and frayed edges.

All of these preliminary activities will create an air of confidence when you enter the classroom.

Systematic Preparation

You will want to develop a structure for your lectures. They shouldn't be simply a flow of information chopped into time chunks. Clarke ("Building a Lecture," p. 52) offers some suggestions that will help you to accomplish this:

- Select your topic.
- Develop a question that serves as a guide. Pose your question at the start of your lecture, then answer it at the end: Recall the question I raised at the beginning of today's class ..., repeat the question, then give a one-statement thesis.
- List the important parts, steps, and elements of the lecture's thesis.
- Collect media items such as charts, maps, photographs, transparencies, and slides that will help communicate the thesis.
- Identify key details to include in the lecture.
- Summarize the thesis. Make a list of important facts, concepts, principles, generalizations, and happenings that contributed in some way to the thesis you are presenting.

Outline the Lecture

An outline of the lecture is essential in several ways:

- It provides a snapshot of the entire lecture. It gives you more confidence and a better idea of how the class session will flow when you review the topic headings and subheadings prior to class time.
- It helps keep you on track.
- It allows you to estimate better how much time will be needed to deliver the lecture.
- You can insert questions at key points in the outline.
- You can give the students copies of the outline to help them follow the lecture and to use when reviewing for quizzes and examinations.
- You can rehearse your lecture while following your outline; you could audiotape record the practice session and make necessary adjustments.

Use facts early in the lecture, and end with higher-level reasoning that leads students to conclusions. By opening the lecture with a thesis question and following with a series of related facts and events that serve as a flight of stairs, you can guide the students as they climb to the higher levels of application, analysis, synthesis, and problem-solving.

The use of questions could stimulate interaction in large classes. Queries with one-word or two-word answers would get the students started. Directing questions to the class in general, instead of singling out individuals to respond, seems the better approach. When a student gives a mumbled response, repeat the answer. In mid-lecture, ask the class to take five minutes to pose questions — and if the questions are good, say so! Near the end of the lecture, direct the students to take two minutes to write out a question over the day's content — one they believe might appear on an examination. Collect and review their questions before the next class session; when you find a good one, use it to modify your next presentation so the students take the two-minute question session seriously.

Establish Rapport With the Class

The success of your lecture might depend on how well you have established the climate of the classroom. Calling students by name, reflecting a positive attitude, using humor, and even taking class pictures can enhance rapport with the class.

Begin to identify as many students by name as possible. You could make a seating chart during the first day of class and write down the names of the students as they introduce themselves. Some instructors like to bring a camera to class and take pictures of the students in groups of five. They then circulate the photos and have the students write their names under their faces. Then the instructors can reference the photographs during lectures. When students raise questions, instructors can call on them by name, building images of the students throughout the semester.

The more positive you can be, the more likely it is that the students will react favorably to your presentations. Positive reinforcement reinforces learning: praise students when they provide very good answers to questions. However, avoid praising everything and praising generically. Some instructors get into the habit of saying "Good answer" or "Good idea" to every comment from their students, who soon realize that the praise is empty.

Studies have shown that humor can increase student attention while providing examples that promote learning (Powell and Andresen, 1985, "Humor and Teaching in Higher Education"). Korobkin, "Humor in the Classroom: Considerations and Strategies" (1988, p. 155), lists several alleged benefits in the use of humor:

- Retention of material.
- Student-teacher rapport.
- Attentiveness and interest.
- Motivation toward and satisfaction with learning.
- Playfulness and positive attitude.
- Individual and group task productivity.
- Class discussion and animation.
- Creativity, idea generation, and divergent thinking.

Korobkin states that humor decreases:

- Academic stress.
- Anxiety toward subject matter.
- Dogmatism.
- Class monotony.

Spontaneous humor between instructors and students is desirable, while malicious humor that ridicules individual students or gender, race, religion, age, appearance, or other differences is wrong.

Studies are revealing the benefits derived when instructors interact with students and when students interact with other students. You can pause during the lecture and ask a question about the content covered during the previous five or 10 minutes. You can break the lecture and have students engage in small group discussions when the lecture has taken them to the edge of a problem-solving situation. These can be refreshing and productive changes of pace for students and you.

Creating a Lively Lecture

When you do it well, the lecture can:

- Impart new information.
- Explain, clarify and organize difficult concepts.
- Model a creative mind at work or the problem-solving process.
- Analyze and show relationships among seemingly dissimilar ideas.
- Inspire a reverence for learning.
- Challenge beliefs and habits of thinking.
- Breed enthusiasm and motivation for further study.

(Frederick, 1986, "The Lively Lecture — 8 Varia-

tions," p. 44).

Frederick claims there are at least eight variations on the lecture that can make it more lively:

1. The Exquisite Oral Essay. This finely tuned presentation deals with one intellectual question or problem, has unity, and is "introduced, illustrated, and concluded within 50 minutes" (p. 45). The instructor conveys only the important information. An example would be a lecture devoted entirely to Robert E. Lee's experiences at the military academy before the Civil War.

2. The Participatory Lecture. During this approach, students are encouraged to develop "ideas which are then organized in some rational, coherent pattern on the chalkboard" (p. 45). The instructor could list the events leading up to the Civil War as the students suggest them. Once the list has been exhausted those items that appear to have similarities could be grouped together. Labels or titles could be created for each group of events — "How would you label these three events?" The groups could be reorganized by titles on a timeline from the earliest set of events to the final group just prior to the outbreak of the Civil War.

3. Problem-Solving: Demonstrations, Proofs, and Stories. Opening with a question can catch students' attention. You then develop the answer throughout the class session. The solution "may require a scientific demonstration, a mathematical proof, an economic model, the outcome of the novel's plot, or an historical narrative" (pp. 46-47). For example, an instructor might begin a lecture with the following: "When Franklin Roosevelt returned from the Yalta Conference near the close of World War II, news films depicted a crew of Secret Service men lifting him out of railway car while he lay on a stretcher. Was he near death? Had he been injured during the return trip from Yalta? Had he been stricken with an illness? Why was he on a stretcher?" The instructor builds the lecture around Roosevelt's early political career, when he was suddenly struck by polio, an illness that caused him to devote much of his effort to eradicating the disease — "The March of Dimes."

4. Energy Shifts: Alternating Mini-Lectures and Discussions. The instructor sets the stage with a 15- to 20-minute lecture, followed by 10-15 minutes of discussion. A new topic is introduced during another 15- to 20-minute lecture, followed by 10-15 minutes of discussion.

The instructor gives the class an assignment at the close of the class session, and the next class session begins with a mini- discussion of that assignment.

5. Textual Exegesis: Modeling Analytical Skills. This approach can be used in courses as varied as the history of art, music, economics, anthropology, science, social science, and English. It is a process of analytical modeling: "A class of 50 or 500 students, following along in their books, or on handouts, or on an overhead projection, can watch a professor working through selected passages of a document, speech, sermon, essay, poem, proof, or fictional passage" (p. 47). For example, an instructor could direct the students to turn to a certain page in the basic textbook, and then the instructor thinks aloud as the students read the page. The instructor demonstrates his learning style by talking as he skims through the page of the text.

6. Cutting Large Classes in Half Without Losing Control: Debates. A classroom of students can be divided into two sides by using a center aisle. Half of the students support one side of an issue while the other half support a different view: "From the right side of the hall we will hear five statements on behalf of the Confederacy, after which we will hear five statements from the left on behalf of the Union" (p. 48). You could even create a middle ground for those students who wish to remain neutral, but you need to encourage this group to defend its neutrality with reasonable explanations. It would be advisable to provide the students with ample background information and materials prior to the day of the debate. I like to inform the students in advance that they must be prepared to defend *both* sides of the issue, so I can postpone until the day of the debate which half of the room will represent which side of the issue.

7. Smaller Groups in Large Classes: Simulations and Role-Playing. After a mini- lecture, organize the students into small groups. Give each group an explicit role and a specific task to pursue. You can conclude the class by incorporating the solutions or suggestions flowing from each group. Or you might instruct the groups to "prepare speeches and see the deliberations through to some conclusion, or to caucus in order to develop strategies, coalitions, and tactics for achieving their goals" (p. 49).

8. Bells and Whistles: The Affective, Emotional Media Lecture. Frederick describes two approaches "designed to evoke an emotional involvement by affective, emotional

learning, an area woefully neglected in college teaching" (p. 49).

One uses a series of dramatic quotations, poems, or lyrics that focus on a specific topic, perhaps read by some theater arts majors. For example, when working with the Pythagorean theorem in mathematics three students could play the roles of Socrates, Meno, and Meno's slave while they read from the dialogues of Plato. The remainder of the students watch how the dialogue unfolds as Socrates demonstrates to Meno how an uneducated slave can be taught a mathematical theorem simply through a series of questions raised by Socrates.

The second uses a slide-tape presentation. I use a form of this approach each spring term in a college curriculum course. I use the strategy during the week that we celebrate Martin Luther King's birthday. I close the class session by announcing that we will discuss teaching ethics as part of the college curriculum during next week's class, and I ask them to listen, watch, and then depart from the classroom without talking, but to remember how the session ended as they prepare for next week's class. I then play an audiotape of King's "I Have a Dream."

Aspects of Delivery

Any of the above variations on the lecture will provide variety and keep students interested in your course. I can give you some final suggestions when using the lecture approach:

- Know your subject matter. You must reflect a knowledge of your discipline. You communicate your interest in the subject by remaining up-to-date. Toss out the old material and keep adding new information.

- Speak slowly, loudly, and clearly, aiming your words at all areas of the room. Students shouldn't have to strain to hear you. Vary the pitch and tone of your voice.

- Look at the students, not at the blackboard, floor, or ceiling. You pick up many cues from the expressions on the faces of the students.

- Constantly pursue answers to questions about what worked, what didn't work, and what might work the next time you deliver the lecture. Reflect on the last class session. Try to revisualize the flow of the lecture and the students' reactions.

- Be prepared — but be alive, spontaneous. There is something positive about spontaneity in the classroom that keeps students attentive. Spontaneity is an art for you to work on. You want to be prepared, but it is possible to be *overprepared* to the point where you squash spontaneity. Provide illustrations and examples from current events.

- Move your body as well as your mouth; don't take up a fixed posture at a podium. Students question the confidence and preparation of instructors who stand with white knuckles at a podium day after day. You may want to seek advice and counsel from instructors in speech communication and theater arts departments.

- Summarize at the end of the lecture.

5 Increasing Student Involvement

The lecture approach lends itself to the presentation of basic facts and basic information. However, when students have the appropriate knowledge base and your objectives need a strategy other than the lecture, there are a number of different approaches. Alternatives to the lecture include:

- discussions
- term papers
- oral reports
- peer groups
- case studies
- simulations and role-play
- multi-media presentations
- blackboard techniques
- field trips
- individualized plans and self-pacing
- lab experiences
- microcomputer programs

Using Discussions to Encourage Interaction

Discussions are best suited for objectives which deal with higher cognitive processes and problem-solving activities. They are usually more motivating than lectures, although a dynamic and well-orchestrated lecture will probably be more motivational than a poorly planned and disorganized discussion. Consider using the discussion approach when your objectives include having students formulate and solve problems, providing students with an opportunity to judge their own perceptions against the perceptions of other students, and using the diverse experiences of the students to accentuate a point.

Instructors may have problems with shy students or students who tend to react more slowly. Hansen, "Suggestions for Seminar Participants" (1987), has a suggestion: "You might ask a question, but offer the student a chance to prepare an answer while the rest of the class discusses something else for, say, five minutes. This combines respect for the student's ability to handle a useful issue with a soothing offer of time to compose the nerves" (p. 59). Of course, the student may miss something important or feel different from the others. As with almost all decisions in the classroom, it's a judgment call.

Cooperative Learning

Cooperative learning is not easy to define; there are many variations, instructional strategies, and classroom activities that deserve to be included in any descriptions of cooperative learning. Miles and Stubblefield, "Learning Groups in Training and Education" (1982), believe group learning is beneficial for students: "Unlike many other techniques, learning groups offer opportunities for learners to be involved actively in the process, to make use of their own experience, and to assume responsibility for their own learning" (p. 311).

Students might:

- Work in small groups to prepare reports, which they would present in the classroom.
- Serve as peer mentors or tutors to help others develop writing skills or conduct science experiments.
- Work with faculty members on research topics.

Whipple, "Collaborative Learning: Recognizing It When We See It" (1987), notes the following characteristics of cooperative learning:

- It involves instructors and students participating in an active learning experience.
- It bridges the chasm between instructor and students if the instructor *collaborates* with the students in the formative stages of the task to be pursued. This promotes active dialogue between instructors and students.
- It involves a sense of community: cooperation takes precedence over competitiveness. Cooperation is an important skill for stu-

dents to acquire before entering the work force. Students should learn to respect the differences that exist among the members of any given group.

- It involves developing information, because cooperation requires the use of interactive processes. "It is a common misconception that collaborative beliefs about knowledge ignore the value of each knower's contribution. Rather, in a collaborative situation involving, say, six persons, there are *seven* distinct knowledges represented — those of each individual and that of the group as a collective entity" (Whipple, p. 5).

- It brings teaching and research together. Classrooms become the research laboratories for creating knowledge.

- It recreates and refashions old knowledge into new forms: the knowledge emerges from the social interactions among the participants, and it lives in the community of students who are involved in cooperative learning.

Some examples of cooperative learning:

A physical chemistry instructor obtained background information from all of the students in the course, then divided them into groups, mixing chemistry and engineering majors. He assigned them a reading, conducted group discussions, tested them, engaged them in group discussions of the test, participated in group activities such as cases and role-playing, and finally presented a culminating lecture.

Some instructors use "learning cells" or "dyads" that stress cooperative learning in pairs. Students read an assignment, then write questions dealing with major facts, concepts, etc. At the beginning of the next class session, the students are randomly assigned to pairs. Partner A asks partner B the first question. After B answers and perhaps receives corrections, B asks A the next question, and so on. The instructor moves from dyad to dyad asking questions and providing feedback.

The success of cooperative learning depends on several factors, including understanding the process, engaging the students in meaningful group activities, and advanced planning before implementing the assignment.

A math instructor tried cooperative learning in a calculus class (Kaiser, 1988). The results were disastrous. Does that sound familiar? We hear or read about new strategies that have been successful for someone else, but then they don't work for us. Well, this math instructor didn't blame the strategy when she failed. She immediately reflected on the experience, and identified the causes for the failure — students were tired, she hadn't prepared them for the activity, and she didn't know how to implement cooperative learning.

She learned more about the process — that small informal work groups spend only five to ten minutes together, while more formal cooperative learning groups worked until a specific job was completed, sometimes for several weeks.

Now armed with basic knowledge, she prepared her students long before she tried cooperative learning again. She told her calculus students they had to read the material before class, and she explained that the class would combine tiny lectures with short tasks to complete in groups of two. When the students completed the assignment, the instructor reported the class session was a great success! She was surprised they managed to cover all the materials they had to cover, and she noted that the students' energy levels were very high throughout the activity. She also received enthusiastic responses from the students when she queried them about their interest in the cooperative learning approach.

She noted, "By using class time to have the partners discuss a new assignment (instead of my lecturing about it), I've noticed a big improvement in the finished programs. And by moving around the room to answer a group's questions and to keep discussions going, I have time to challenge the brighter students and encourage the slower students without embarrassing anyone" (Kaiser, p. 3).

She also reported another interesting observation. She claimed that those students who were enrolled in calculus only because there wasn't any other course were slightly unhappy — they discovered that they had to *participate* instead of just *passing time* in her classroom!

Critical Thinking

Browne and Keeley, "Do College Students Know How to 'Think Critically' When They Graduate?" (1988), declare that many students lack critical thinking skills, concluding, "To improve the thinking skills of students, professors should be aware that the traditional curricula do not guarantee the internalization of critical thinking skills. Direct training, combined with practice and reinforcement, is needed to facilitate the development of critical thinking skills" (p. 2).

Can we assess critical thinking if we can't see it? We can observe learners' critical thinking behavior as reflected during a classroom discussion. We can critique students' products generated by critical thinking outside the classroom, such as a term paper. Critical thinking might be reflected in the development of three-dimensional models.

According to Brookfield, *Developing Critical Thinkers: Challenging Adults to Explore Alternative Ways of Thinking and Acting* (1987), critical thinking involves the dual processes of "identifying and challenging assumptions" and "imagining and exploring alternatives" (p. 229). That is far from being a passive activity.

Brookfield's theory incorporates the following generalizations about critical thinking (pp. 231-233):

- The processes involved are person-specific.
- Emotions play a major role.
- Both intrinsic and extrinsic reasons are important.
- It can occur unexpectedly.
- Peer support is important.

There are many ways to encourage students to develop critical thinking skills. Brookfield provides an excellent set of conclusions to help guide us in facilitating critical thinking (pp. 233-235):

- No *one* model of critical thinking stands out as a panacea; intervening variables involving people and contexts negate the possibility of one standard model for everyone.
- We must provide a variety of methods and materials for diverse learners.
- We shouldn't expect perfection.
- We shouldn't look at "learner satisfaction" as the primary criterion for judging the level of success of a critical thinking activity — sometimes we need periods of frustration, and sometimes we need to struggle to find potential solutions to problems.
- We need to take risks, which entail the possibility of failure, but we should not stop our efforts simply because of one attempt that's less than successful.

Field Studies

Field study methodology, according to Wulff and Nyquist, "Using Field Methods as an Instructional Tool" (1988), is an instructional tool that sharpens critical thinking. Field studies are usually long-term and are not the same as short field trips. Students "observe, analyze, classify and report human behavior occurring in natural environments" (p. 87).

Wulff and Nyquist describe one approach to field study. The instructor had students compare and contrast the findings from their observations with those from readings and lectures. Students were to present tentative hypotheses and conclusions to their peers. The activity included small group discussions and encouraged synthesis.

The instructor wanted the students to perform as researchers, and arranged for a presentation by a researcher experienced in field methods. The presentation included information on taking notes in the field, what to include in the record, separating observations and inferences, formulating hypotheses, analyzing and classifying information into categories, identifying themes, and presenting and supporting conclusions with specific findings from field notes (p. 91).

Hess, "Thinking about Thinking: Bloom's Taxonomy Rediscovered" (1988), engages her business students in thinking about thinking exercises. She believes such experiences are essential if business students are to succeed in the real world. In her effort to discover protocols that identify steps, skills, processes, and behaviors involved in reasoning, decision-making, problem-solving, learning-to-learn, and critical and creative thinking, she rediscovered the *Taxonomy of Educational Objectives* (Bloom et al., 1956).

When Hess introduces some course content, she has the students reference a handout on which the following six levels of the cognitive domain are listed:

- knowledge
- comprehension
- application
- analysis
- synthesis
- evaluation

The handout includes "a key word, a thinking process, teaching goals, student behaviors, and typical words ... that require thinking at that level" (p. 2). The students read the handout and then think about each of Bloom's levels, which are then demonstrated by the instructor and practiced by the students.

Browne and Keeley, "Do College Students Know How to 'Think Critically' When They Graduate?" (1988), asked a group of students to evaluate a 550-word essay. The essay had many errors of evidence, ambiguities, and assumptions, as well as important missing information. More than 50% did not question any of the ambiguities, and more than 50% failed to comment on a loose definition that was essential for the students to be able to draw accurate conclusions about the article.

Powers and Enright, "Analytical Reasoning Skills in Graduate Study" (1987), wanted to identify those reasoning skills perceived by faculty as most critical for students to succeed in graduate schools. They noted that when faculty members were asked to identify important reasoning skills, the most highly rated critical thinking skills involved reasoning or problem-solving when needed information was not known, the ability to identify fallacies and contradictions in arguments, and noting similarities between types of problems or theories. They also identified the three more serious errors in reasoning: inability to question assumptions, inability to integrate and synthesize the ideas obtained from a variety of sources, and inability to develop hypotheses independently.

In my "College Teaching" course, I provide a simulation experience during which the students are identified as first-year assistant professors at my institution; I serve as their department chair, regardless of the students' disciplines. I provide the students with real catalogues, rules and regulations, policy manuals, etc., and then I give them a set of 20 "in-basket" items that are typical problems that all new instructors must handle. The students have one hour to write down their courses of action with the "in-basket" items: if they make phone calls, they must write out the conversation; if they want to send the secretary a note, they must write out the note; if they need to talk to me, they discover that I am in Houston and can't be reached " therefore, they write out their actions. Eventually the entire group of students is engaged in discussing the more critical issues they will probably confront in the real world.

It's very rewarding to observe the discussions, and I always prod here and there to force students to reveal their decision-making processes. They soon begin to learn that critical thinking takes place within a context, that there are alternative courses of action that should be explored, that reflecting about and probing into others' reasons for actions can lead to valuable lessons, and that data collection precedes conclusions.

A team of researchers at the National Center for Research to Improve Postsecondary Teaching and Learning (NCRIPTAL) developed a self-report instrument to evaluate the motivational orientation and learning strategies of college students; see Pintrich et al., *Motivated Strategies for Learning Questionnaire* (MSLQ), 1988. One section of the instrument deals with critical thinking. We can duplicate and distribute that section to our students, and we can take time to elaborate on the items during class time:

- When confronted with difficult problems, try to develop potential solutions — and then check out your hypothesized answers.

- When instructors present theories and generalizations, try to find supporting evidence.

- When you read or hear an assertion or conclusion, think about potential alternatives.

- Instead of relying entirely on the instructor's ideas, develop your own understanding of topics you read or hear.

Using Questions to Enhance Discussions

One of the criticisms identified with classroom instruction is the failure of some teachers to engage students in the use of higher cognitive processes — to think. Earlier I mentioned a taxonomy of educational objectives that presented six levels of cognition: knowledge, comprehension, application, analysis, synthesis, and evaluation (Bloom et al., 1956). Four are usually considered to be at the higher level of the cognitive domain: application, analysis, synthesis, evaluation. You can use those four levels of the taxonomy to guide you in developing questions to enhance discussions and engage students in thinking.

Application questions. These questions have a broader scope than simple recall of information, and they can be applied to a variety of contexts:

- "Having read the *Dialogues of Plato,* how can you apply the teaching style of Socrates in your own classroom instruction?"

- "Having discussed the research findings at the Hawthorne Plant of Western Electric, how would you behave as an administrator or manager in a similar plant where they might mass produce light fixtures?"

The purpose of such questions is to lead students to apply concepts, principles, or generalizations in different contexts.

Questions that call for analysis and synthesis. These questions require students to draw on the knowledge they have learned in order to apply that knowledge to a given situation:

- "Why does cotton grow better in the Brazos Valley than in the higher areas of the Big Bend country?"
- "What could a builder do with the land around the intersection of Highway 6 and Highway 10 if the swamps were drained?"

Questions that require students to compare two objects or statements force students to look for similarities and differences:

- "How does the HWP Laserjet II differ from the IBM QuietWriter Printer Model 2?"
- "Are the editorials on the topic of energy different in the *New York Times* and the *Houston Chronicle?* Explain."

Questions that call for evaluation. Most of the time there are no specific right or wrong answers for evaluation questions, and that makes the standards or criteria the instructor will use to judge the students' responses an important part of prepresentation strategy:

- Look at these two microscopes. Which is the better instrument, and why?
- Was U.S. Grant a better general than Robert E. Lee, and why?

Bloom contends that evaluation requires students to use some combination of cognitive processes listed earlier — knowledge, comprehension, application, analysis and synthesis.

Problem-solving questions. Problem-solving questions enable students to use their creativity in devising solutions to problems. It is this active involvement that enables students to more easily store information in long-term memory. Active involvement may also make it easier for students to *retrieve* information from long-term memory at a later date. For example:

- "I want you to form groups of five, and I want you to reference your notes and the new handouts I distributed today. During the next 30 minutes I want your group to reach a consensus about the following question: How would you go about developing a new shopping center in this community?"
- "The U.S. Supreme Court has ruled that our state must develop a plan that reveals a more equitable distribution of funding to finance public education for students enrolled in our elementary and secondary schools. How would you propose to solve the problem?"

Probing questions. One of the key strategies for engaging students in discussions is to use probing questions — add this to your repertoire. It involves the use of the word "Why?" Use this probing question when you have raised an initial question and the student has given you a "Yes"/ "No" or simplistic response. This forces the student to go beyond surface responses to your questions. In responding to a "Why?" question, the student must reveal thought processes, knowledge bases, sources of information, and the ability to *think* above the recall and comprehension levels.

Integrating Cooperative Learning and Critical Thinking

An instructor could organize the class into small groups and then assign problems to the groups so they use a technique entitled "Documented Problem-Set Solutions" (Cross and Angelo, *Classroom Assessment Techniques: A Handbook for Faculty,* 1988). The purpose of the technique is to have group members actually *document in writing* the steps they take in solving their problems, and to share their steps with the class at the close of the activity, so the instructor can assess their problem-solving methods.

Students or groups could also trade papers and analyze each other's steps or each group's steps noted in solving the problems. Cross and Angelo believe the technique can be used in such diverse areas as accounting, algebra, calculus, statistics, law, organic chemistry, grammar, music, and computer programming. The instructor develops an initial set of problems for the groups to solve, then uses a variety of questions throughout the entire problem-solving experience, thus integrating cooperative learning, critical thinking, and the use of questions.

6   CIAS: Enhancing Discussion

I've developed a Cognitive Interaction Analysis System (CIAS) that enhances the use of discussions (Johnson, "Changing the Verbal Behavior of Teachers," 1987). If we accept the idea that teaching and learning involve at least to some extent the reciprocal, interdependent communication between two or more people (teacher and learners), we can study one set of variables — verbal interactions — and help you analyze this phase of your teaching and the learning by students.

When students are encouraged to interact with each other in an orderly manner, thinking occurs because one student's contribution builds upon another student's contribution under the guidance of the classroom instructor.

Interaction analysis involves coding classroom verbal statements, organizing the coded data, displaying the data in a useful way, and inferring conclusions about your teaching and the learning by your students that took place during a lesson.

I started by developing a set of 10 categories to use for all of the verbal statements that take place in college classrooms. Next, I developed descriptions of the categories and examples of each category, as well as a set of ground rules to guide the observers. I then assigned numerals to each of the 10 categories. Users of the system are trained to record the classroom interaction, i.e., they listen to a number of audiotaped class segments until they memorize the categories and the numeral for each category, and then they write down the correct numeral each time the instructor uses a category. The data are converted to a matrix format that enables the instructor to interpret the flow of the verbal interaction that took place in the classroom. This procedure is very similar to one developed by Flanders, *Analyzing Teaching Behavior* (1970, pp. 28-29).

I believe if you train yourself in using interaction analysis you'll enhance your verbal behavior in the classroom. In fact, my studies have supported my contention. Research studies have revealed significant changes in the verbal behavior of instructors, accompanied by increased student learning, when instructors applied

interaction analysis (Johnson, "Delphi-Process Evaluation of the Effectiveness of Selected In-Service Training Techniques to Improve Community/Junior College Instruction," 1976; Johnson, "An Eclectic Systematic Instruction Model for Expository Instruction," 1987; Johnson, "Changing the Verbal Behavior of Teachers," 1987; Vietor, Brubaker, Milford, and Johnson, "Teacher Improvement Using a Cognitive Interaction Analysis System," 1985).

Expository Teaching (ET) is also enhanced when you learn an interaction analysis system. ET involves selecting, organizing, translating, and presenting content in a flexible manner during a supervised unit of study when teacher-student and student-student interactions are encouraged throughout the delivery of the subject matter.

After mastering the system you can record verbal communication in your classrooms, then analyze your teaching by using the procedures I will describe.

College instructors who were trained in interaction analysis found that the training was useful in their teaching (Johnson, "Delphi-Process Evaluation of the Effectiveness of Selected In-Service Training Techniques to Improve Community/Junior College Instruction," 1976). The use of interaction analysis has increased awareness of inconsistencies between instructional goals and cognitive behavior (Vietor, Brubaker, Milford, and Johnson, "Teacher Improvement Using a Cognitive Interaction Analysis System," 1985).

Perhaps I should briefly mention the work of Bloom (1976), since his research had a direct influence on me to include his findings within four of the 10 categories. Bloom identified four major elements he identified with quality of instruction:

- **Cues** provided by the instructor.
- **Participation** by the students.
- **Reinforcement** techniques used by the instructor.
- **Corrective/feedback** provided by the instructor.

The CIAS has 10 categories. The first seven categories represent *teacher talk*, while two are for *student talk* and one for silent pauses of three or more seconds.

Category 1: Instructor Accepts Student Attitudes

Identify as Category 1 non-threatening comments by the instructor that express accept ance of students' attitudes — even if those attitudes are negative. Instead of attacking or criticizing students who express negative feelings during the course, instructors should communicate that they recognize students' negative attitudes. This approach prevents embarrassing situations.

The attitudes of the students may be either negative or positive. An instructor may support positive attitudes as follows: "All of you appear to be very confident about tomorrow's quiz, and I'm sure you will do well." An example of accepting negative attitudes would be: "You appear to be upset about the grades."

Jokes and humorous stories told by the instructor are also recorded as Category 1.

The use of Category 1 is rare in college classrooms. My students compiled over 39,000 tallies of verbal interaction from 48 different classrooms, and only one-tenth of 1% of the total tallies fell into Category 1. Perhaps instructors haven't paid enough attention to the power of this type of verbal behavior. They may not have their antennae up for student input. This is a skill you should develop as a beginning instructor.

Category 2: Instructor Uses Positive Reinforcement

Identify as Category 2 any instructor statement that communicates a definite value judgment, indicating that he/she likes what the student said or did. For example: "Excellent! That's a great suggestion!"

Almost every theorist has supported reinforcement as a way to facilitate learning (Bergan and Dunn, *Psychology and Education: A Science for Instruction*, 1976, p. 212). Responses followed by rewards strengthens learning (Bugelski, *The Psychology of Learning Applied to Teaching*, 1971, pp. 57-58). "Learning takes place only when the act that is performed is reinforced" (Symonds, *What Education Has to Learn From Psychology*, 1968, p. 11).

Powerful extrinsic reinforcers, such as verbal praise by the instructor, can be a valuable tool for learning. One caution: don't overuse positive statements. They must be appropriate reactions. In fact, once learning is progressing well within a unit of study, it may be advisable to reduce or omit reinforcers from time to time (Bugelski, *The Psychology of Learning Applied to Teaching*, 1971, p. 96).

Keep in mind that an instructor's statement is categorized as a positive reinforcer only if his/her voice communicates enthusiasm and expresses that he/she likes the student's response or action. If this is not clearly signaled, the statement is probably a Category 3.

Category 3: Instructor Uses Corrections or Provides Feedback

These statements are non-punitive and non-threatening, such as "No" or "Yes" or "That's correct." If the instructor merely repeats a student's correct response so that all students know the answer was correct or acceptable, use Category 3 as depicted in the following:

Student: "Abe Lincoln."
Teacher: "Abe Lincoln" (Category 3) or "Yes, John, that is the correct answer" (Category 3).

Category 3 is used when the instructor's voice does not communicate a value judgment of liking the student's response. Compare the following:

Student: "Abe Lincoln."
Teacher: "Abe Lincoln!" (Category 2) or "Yes, that's great!" (Category 2).

Rosenshine (1976) reviewed research studies which involved corrective/feedback. He reported that "19 of the 20 correlations were positive, and 13 were significant. This positive correlation held regardless of the type of feedback, that is, even for negative feedback. ... Such results suggest that the *topic* of feedback ... is more important than the *type* of feedback" (p. 361).

Symonds (1968) referenced the works of Thorndike and Skinner, indicating that the use of the word "wrong" had no negative impact on learning if the teacher's tone wasn't harsh (p. 29). He noted that an experiment by Hurlock revealed that praise was three to four times superior to reproof, but Symonds also believed that both forms served as incentives in learning (p. 31). He thought that a very mild punishment didn't actually hurt the individual, and that any anxiety would hardly be recognizable. Yet, the anxiety would provide a signal to the learner to guide behavior and responses (p. 31).

We don't want students to leave our classrooms with wrong understandings as their last remembrances. Therefore, I think we need to employ more corrections and provide more feedback during class time, so students don't depart with misunderstandings.

Category 4: Instructor Asks Questions

Identify as Category 4 any question, including rhetorical questions, and when the instructor rephrases a student's comment in the form of a question:

Student: "It's a desolate area and would deter growth potential."

Teacher: "Are you saying that the location is removed from modes of transportation?" (Category 4).

The instructor's questions are important to student learning. Studies have revealed positive and significant correlations between instructors' questions and students' achievement, when direct questions focus on academics.

We ask questions to invite students to participate and to contribute their ideas, opinions, or knowledge. Gall and Gall, "The Discussion Method" (1976), indicated that the instructor's questions promoted learning even for those who just listened to the discussion while engaging in convergent learning (p. 210). Responses to the instructor's questions can provide feedback opportunities for students and instructors. Some teachers ask questions at the beginning of a class session to determine the progress students are making, so responses serve as information the instructor can use to move the students toward desired objectives (Shavelson, "Teachers' Decision-Making," 1976, p. 412).

Category 5: Instructor Lectures

Identify as Category 5 instructor talk that communicates facts, expresses ideas, or provides illustrations. Category 5 usually has the highest frequency of tallies of all 10 categories. Of the 39,000 tallies recorded in various classrooms, my students identified almost two-thirds as Category 5; in some disciplines, more than 70% of the tallies were recorded as Category 5. Lecture is the primary mode of presenting basic subject matter, therefore, the predominance of tallies in Category 5 should come as no surprise.

Category 6: Instructor Gives Cues or Directions

Identify as Category 6 words that signal importance — "This is important to remember; record it in your notebooks" — and statements that require students to do something — "John, give me the answer to problem 43" or "Look at the five genres of literature I have listed on the blackboard. Keep them in mind throughout the lesson." Cues or directions may appear anytime during a lesson, and several cues/directions may be interspersed throughout the lesson.

Many descriptions of cues create problems for people who are recording interaction analysis; they struggle with beginning and ending parts of statements and find overlap with other categories of interaction if the definition of a cue is restrictive.

Bloom, *Human Characteristics and School Learning* (1976), provided the following help: "Cues may be relatively simple, such as a sound or word to be related to a particular object, event, or activity; the relating of a particular signal; the demonstration of a sequence of physical activity; or the directions for a complex set of cognitive processes" (p. 115).

For CIAS, cues and directions are verbal signals to pay attention to what is about to follow or to react to something. I combine directions and cues because giving directions is related to cuing. Cues gain the attention of the listener. They highlight events. After highlighting or giving procedural directions (Category 6), instructors usually return to presenting more information to the students (Category 5).

Category 7: Instructor Criticizes Students

Identify as Category 7 any negative, punitive comments, strong criticism, and blame:

"Ridiculous."

"That's silly."

"Don't interrupt me when I'm giving my lectures."

Although CIAS attaches no rating or value scale to each category, Category 7 should be avoided as much as possible. Blame or a feeling of failure inflict a kind of pain. Many students can describe the feeling of helplessness that grabbed them when an instructor rendered an intensive verbal attack. Instead of responding with thoughtful contributions, they froze or repeated their original, erroneous answers.

Smith, *Research in Teacher Education: A Symposium* (1971), reviewed several studies and reported that "the stronger forms of criticism had a higher negative correlation with achievement than the milder form. Thus, teachers who use extreme amounts of criticism usually have classes which achieve less in most subject areas" (pp. 50-51).

Category 8: Cognitive Student Talk

Identify as Category 8 student talk that is oriented around subject matter:

- Recalling facts.
- Responding to teacher questions or directions with subject matter responses or questions.
- Expressing opinions or ideas about topics under study.
- Analyzing, synthesizing, or evaluating.

Cognitive student talk can be viewed as a form of participation and/or recitation. Students are responding when they talk, and they are learning. Various studies on recitation support this viewpoint (Bloom, *Human Characteristics and School Learning*, 1976; Symonds, *What Education Has to Learn From Psychology*, 1968).

Category 9: Non-Cognitive Student Talk

Identify as Category 9 student talk that is *not* related to subject matter:
"Can we leave now?"
"Can we take a break?"
"I went to the basketball game last night."
"Is the quiz tomorrow instead of Friday?"
Category 9 accounts for probably less than 1% of the total tallies recorded in most classrooms.

Category 0: Silence

Identify as Category 0 pauses of three full seconds or longer when there is no verbal communication or when communication can't be understood. Silence occurs when students are reflecting or reading silently, when the instructor is rearranging some equipment for a demonstration or writing on the board silently.

For a Category 0 to be recorded, the silence

must be a full three seconds or more. (This is the only category of CIAS where each tally must be a full three seconds before it can be recorded.) We use a zero rather than 10 because it is easier and quicker to write, and more convenient when using the computer program to produce CIAS printouts.

All 10 categories of CIAS are summarized in Figure 1 (see page 35).

Procedures for Recording CIAS

Once the observer (that's you if you're replaying an audiotape of your lesson) feels comfortable and notes that the lesson is underway, he/she records the time, writes down a zero to begin, and at the close of each three seconds decides which category best represents the interaction that took place during that three-second period. The observer continues, writing the category numbers in sequence *one by one* until the lesson is completed. It is important for the observer to record a zero to begin the lesson and a zero at the end of the lesson. These two zeros, in contrast to other zeros recorded during the lesson, are used to show the opening and the closing of the lesson.

You will probably feel overwhelmed during the first two or three hours of training. That's normal. I have trained thousands of people in interaction analysis, and every one experienced the same frustration during the first few hours of skill practice. But 99% became excellent recorders of interaction analysis. You, too, will develop the timing and expertise in recording interaction analysis every three seconds after you have memorized the 10 categories, learned the ground rules, and practiced for a few hours. Hang in there! It is like any other skill: practice makes perfect.

Ground Rules for Recording CIAS

1. Do not record CIAS during the opening of the class session when the instructor is dealing with management tasks instead of cognitive aspects of the lesson (e.g., checking attendance, collecting assignments, returning tests).

2. Begin to record CIAS when the instructor and/or students engage in cognitive aspects of the lesson. Even students can initiate the interaction, e.g., a student might raise his/her hand and ask, "Last time you talked about _____. What did you mean?"

3. Record the numeral representing the

Figure 1

Cognitive Interaction Analysis System Categories

No rating scale is implied; the numerals merely indicate the particular category of interaction in use during each three seconds.

Silence Category (0)

Category 0 — Silence: Three seconds or more of silence; pauses when no communication exists for three seconds or more; noisy confusion when it is not possible to decipher the talk taking place, such as when students are noisy while rearranging the room for group activities.

Teacher Talk Categories (1-7)

Category 1 — Accepting Student Attitudes: Comments that communicate a non-threatening acceptance of student attitudes, which may be positive or negative, i.e., "You appear to be upset about this" or "I'm glad to see all are happy about the results from last week's test."

Category 2 — Positive Reinforcement: Praising students; communicating a definite value judgment indicating that the instructor likes what the student said or did, i.e., "Excellent!" or "Very good!"

Category 3 — Correction or Feedback: Includes negative statements which are nonpunitive and nonthreatening; saying "no" or "yes" or "that's correct" in a manner that provides feedback to students; repeating a student's response so all students know the answer was correct or acceptable.

Category 4 — Questions: Includes rhetorical questions; all questions raised by the teacher; calling on students by name *if* the student has raised his/her hand to respond to a question.

Category 5 — Lecture: Communicating facts, expressing ideas, giving examples, providing illustrations.

Category 6 — Providing Cues or Directions: Words that signal importance: "This is *important* to remember!" "These next four items may appear on your final examination in the course." Directions the instructor expects the students to follow, including procedural direction; calling a student's name with the purpose of directing him/her to respond.

Category 7 — Criticism: Negative, punitive comments; strong criticism; blaming students; saying "Ridiculous" or "That's silly" or "Don't interrupt me like that when I'm giving my lecture."

Student Talk Categories (8-9)

Category 8 — Cognitive Student Talk: Talk by students which is subject-matter oriented; recalling facts; responding to teacher questions or directions with subject matter responses or subject matter questions; expressing opinions or ideas about topics under study; analyzing, synthesizing, evaluating; subject-matter questions raised by students.

Category 9 — Non-Cognitive Student Talk: Talk by students which is not related to subject matter; management comments by students — "Can we leave now?" "Will we have the quiz tomorrow?" "I went to the game Saturday and didn't have time to prepare my paper."

interaction category once every three seconds.

4. If more than one category of interaction is in evidence during a three-second period, record each category.

5. Except when beginning and ending a lesson, record a zero only when there is a total of three seconds of silence, confusion, or unrecordable noise.

6. Do not use the CIAS if the class views a 16mm sound film, listens to a lengthy audiotape, or spends the class time in silent reading. Merely record the time and write a comment describing the situation. Wait until the instructor is again engaged in cognitive verbal interaction.

7. When in doubt, record the category that is congruent with the predominant mood. For example, if the situation isn't a clear Category 2 or Category 3, think about the previous statements. If the instructor has consistently accepted student responses by repeating or rewording them instead of enthusiastically praising them, record a 3.

8. If you have very long periods of time when communication is undecipherable or when there's chaos, stop recording zeros and write a comment and the time. When the class settles and cognitive interaction resumes, note the time and begin recording again.

9. When the instructor is interacting with several students during a planned cognitive lesson and some students are ignoring the instructor by chatting among themselves, record CIAS for the verbal interaction between the instructor and the students, and ignore those chatting. If, however, the class becomes disruptive and it is apparent that the instructor is disorganized, stop recording, note the time, and write a comment.

Here is an example of the first and last 15 seconds of a lesson:

9:03 a.m.

0 (To mark the start. This zero is not included as part of the verbal interaction during the first 15 seconds; it signals the beginning of the recording of interaction analysis.)

5
5
0
5
5
... (End of first 15 seconds of lesson.)
4
8
8
0

6

0 (End of last 15 seconds of lesson. The last zero is not included as part of the verbal interaction during the last 15 seconds, it signals the end of the recording of interaction analysis.)

By now you have recognized some of the limitations of CIAS. Good! CIAS doesn't provide data about management techniques, isn't appropriate for independent study settings, and doesn't indicate the type of questions the instructor asks.

Matrices

Now that you've sequentially recorded the categories, how do you interpret your data?

Either manually or by computer (I prefer a computer program since it is so much easier and quicker), transfer the numerals to a 10 x 10 matrix. Pair each numeral with the following. For example, for the sequence 0 3 6 4 8, we have the following pairs: 0-3 3-6 6-4 4-8. The first numeral of each pair designates the *row*, while the second numeral of the pair designates the *column*. The tally is marked (placed) on the matrix where the row and column intersect; e.g., a tally in the 3-6 cell means a 3 was followed by a 6. Then the last numeral of the previous tally is paired with the next numeral recorded to form the new pair (see below):

3
    (first pair: 3 and 6)
6
    (second pair: 6 and 4)
4
    (third pair: 4 and 8)
8

Look at Figure 2 (see p. 37). The above three pairs are represented by a tally mark (/) in row 3, column 6; a tally mark in row 6, column 4; and a tally mark in row 4, column 8.

The actual data will be transposed into tallies appearing within the 100 cells of the 10 x 10 matrix. The computer program totals the tallies in each cell; if you are doing this manually, you have to count your tallies in each cell after completing the matrix.

Analysis

You are now ready to analyze the completed matrix. Look for cells with heavy concentrations of tallies. Those represent the most-used categories of CIAS during your lesson.

Figure 2

Category	0	1	2	3	4	5	6	7	8	9
0										
1										
2										
3							(/)			
4									(/)	
5										
6					(/)					
7										
8										
9										

The shaded areas in Figure 3 (see page 38) show a pattern where the instructor asks a question, the student responds to the question, and the instructor provides corrective/feedback.

The shaded areas in Figure 4 (see page 39) show a pattern where the instructor asks a question, the student responds to the question, and the instructor provides reinforcement.

If you want to know the kind of categories that preceded harsh criticism by the instructor, you would look down the 7 column (excluding the 7-7 cell). If one or more tallies appear in the 6-7 cell, you know that cues/directions preceded harsh criticism. If one or more tallies appear in the 10-7 cell, you know that silence preceded the harsh criticism. You exclude the 7-7 cell because the 7-7 cell indicated the use of criticism for more than three consecutive seconds, and the 7-7 cell doesn't tell you which category preceded or followed the 7's.

Conversely, if you want to know the kind of categories that follow an instructor's question, you will look along the 4 row (excluding the 4-4 cell). If several tallies appear in the 4-8 cell, you know the number of times students responded immediately to the instructor's questions.

Frequencies, Ratios, and Percentages

Look at Figure 5 (see page 40). The matrix displays the data collected by one observer using CIAS during an English class. The lesson was about 31 minutes long (one tally recorded every three seconds; 620 tallies times three seconds for each tally = 1860 seconds divided by 60 seconds = 31 minutes). It has a total of 620 tallies.

The following formulas allow you to interpret the matrix in Figure 5.

1. SC (silence) indicates the percent of the *total* time devoted to silence (each three seconds of silence). It is calculated by taking the total number of tallies in either *row* 0 or *column* 0 (they have the same total) and dividing by the total number of all tallies for either all of the *rows* or all of the *columns* in the total matrix.

2. TT (teacher talk) indicates the percent of the total time the instructor talked. It is calculated by taking the sum of Categories 1 + 2 + 3 +

Figure 3

Category	0	1	2	3	4	5	6	7	8	9
0										
1										
2										
3										
4					▨				▨	
5										
6										
7										
8				▨					▨	
9										

The shaded areas show a pattern where the instructor asks a question, the student responds, and the instructor provides corrective/feedback.

4 + 5 + 6 + 7 in either their *rows* or their *columns* and dividing by the total number of tallies for either all of the *rows* or all of the *columns* in the total matrix.

3. PT (pupil talk) indicates the percent of the total time the students talked. It is calculated by taking the sum of Categories 8 + 9 in either their *rows* or their *columns* and dividing by the total number of tallies for either all of the *rows* or all of the *columns* in the total matrix.

4. PTC (pupil talk cognitive) indicates the amount of total student talk that involved cognitive aspects of the lesson. It is calculated by taking the sum of Category 8 in either *row* 8 or *column* 8 and dividing by the total number of tallies for Categories 8 + 9 in either their *rows* or their *columns*.

5. PSSR (total amount of student talk in the same category for more than three seconds, but combining these totals for Categories 8 and 9) is calculated by taking all the tallies in the 8-8 cell plus all the tallies in the 9-9 cell and dividing by the total number of tallies for Categories 8 + 9 in either their *rows* or *columns*.

6. TSSR (teacher talk in the same category for more than three seconds) is calculated by taking all the tallies in cells 1-1, 2-2, 3-3, 4-4, 5-5, 6-6, 7-7 and dividing by the total number of tallies for Categories 1-7 in either their *rows* or *columns*.

7. Q (questions) is a fairly accurate inference about the total number of different times the instructor asks questions. Q is calculated by taking the sum of Category 4 in either the Category 4 *row* or the Category 4 *column* and subtracting the tallies in the 4-4 cell.

8. CF (corrective/feedback) is a fairly accurate inference about the total number of times the instructor provides corrective/feedback to student talk. CF is calculated by taking the sum of Category 3 in either the Category 3 *row* or the Category 3 *column* and subtracting the tallies in the 3-3 cell.

9. R (positive reinforcement) is a fairly accurate inference about the total number of times students receive positive reinforcement from the instructor. R is calculated by taking the sum of Category 2, in either the Category 2 *row* or the

Figure 4

Category	0	1	2	3	4	5	6	7	8	9
0										
1										
2										
3										
4										
5										
6										
7										
8										
9										

The shaded areas show a pattern where the instructor asks a question, the student responds, and the instructor provides reinforcement.

Category 2 *column,* and subtracting the tallies in the 2-2 cell.

You can now analyze the matrix located in Figure 5.

Silence accounted for approximately 4% of the total time: SC = 22 (tallies in either row 0 or column 0) divided by 620 (total tallies) = 3.54%.

What percent of the total time was devoted to instructor talk? The instructor talked about 80% of the total time: TT = 497 (tallies in Categories 1-7) divided by 620 (total tallies) = 80.16%.

What percent of the total time was devoted to student talk? The students talked about 16% of the total time: PT = 101 (tallies in Categories 8 and 9) divided by 620 (total tallies) = 16.29%.

We can also discover the number of times the instructor asked questions, the number of times the instructor used corrective/feedback, and the number of times the instructor used positive reinforcers.

How many questions did the instructor ask? The instructor raised 81 questions during the lesson: Q = 173 (tallies in Category 4) minus 92 (tallies in the 4-4 cell) = 81.

It seems fair to conclude that the instructor used a Socratic approach during the lesson.

How many times did the instructor make corrections or provide feedback to the students? The instructor used 53 different correction and feedback statements: CF = 68 (tallies in Category 3) minus 15 (tallies in the 3-3 cell) = 53.

This was advisable when dealing with content that was a new topic for the students. The Category 3 tallies were prompted by the large number of instructor questions followed by student responses which the instructor used to provide corrective/feedback.

How often did the instructor use positive reinforcement? The instructor used 16 positive reinforcement statements: R = 18 (tallies in Category 2) minus 2 (tallies in the 2-2 cell) = 16. Since the content was new for the students, the instructor was wise to provide positive reinforcement to the students as they responded with correct answers to his questions. This would help to build the confidence of the students as they explored the new content.

All of the student talk was cognitive: PTC =

Figure 5

Matrix of Pairs

	0	1	2	3	4	5	6	7	8	9
0	3	0	0	0	5	6	3	0	5	0
1	0	6	0	0	2	1	1	0	1	0
2	0	0	2	0	8	5	2	0	1	0
3	1	1	7	15	23	13	6	0	2	0
4	10	2	0	1	92	5	5	0	58	0
5	1	0	2	3	22	94	7	0	1	0
6	7	0	1	0	12	4	73	0	0	0
7	0	0	0	0	0	0	0	0	0	0
8	0	2	6	49	9	2	0	0	33	0
9	0	0	0	0	0	0	0	0	0	0
SUM	22	11	18	68	173	130	97	0	101	0

Percentages for Observations

	0	1	2	3	4	5	6	7	8	9
0	0.5%	0.0%	0.0%	0.0%	0.8%	1.0%	0.5%	0.0%	0.8%	0.0%
1	0.0 %	1.0%	0.0%	0.0%	0.3%	0.2%	0.2%	0.0%	0.2%	0.0%
2	0.0%	0.0%	0.3%	0.0%	1.3%	0.8%	0.3%	0.0%	0.2%	0.0%
3	0.2%	0.2%	1.1%	2.4%	3.7%	2.1%	1.0%	0.0%	0.3%	0.0%
4	1.6%	0.3%	0.0%	0.2%	14.8%	0.8%	0.8%	0.0%	9.4%	0.0%
5	0.2%	0.0%	0.3%	0.5%	3.5%	15.2%	1.1%	0.0%	0.2%	0.0%
6	1.1%	0.0%	0.2%	0.0%	1.9%	0.6%	11.8%	0.0%	0.0%	0.0%
7	0.0%	0.0%	0.0%	0.0%	0.0%	0.0%	0.0%	0.0%	0.0%	0.0%
8	0.0%	0.3%	1.0%	7.9%	1.5%	0.3%	0.0%	0.0%	5.3%	0.0%
9	0.0%	0.0%	0.0%	0.0%	0.0%	0.0%	0.0%	0.0%	0.0%	0.0%
SUM	3.5%	1.8%	2.9%	11.0%	27.9%	21.0%	15.6%	0.0%	16.3%	0.0%

Final Results

Q	=	81	CF	=	53	R	=	16
SC	=	3.55%	TT	=	80.16%	PT	=	16.29%
PTC	=	100.00%	PSSR	=	32.67%	TSSR	=	56.74%

Original Input Data

0555544444	4843483483	4484484834	8483541144	8334883444
8118348883	3554441155	5483334006	2448488883	4489444448
3444448336	4444454488	8322555556	6666648483	5544834834
8483666644	8348348348	3555544448	4883488324	8324836644
4440444828	3444583348	3244888883	2555555555	6666555554
4882555555	6666660483	3344883554	0835354008	8255555260
0555483354	8354885524	8333455644	4448833388	8324444482
2536660555	5555555555	5555483835	4444488834	4448324455
4483364404	4466666655	5555555605	5445554088	8833554665
5550556555	4040554483	5555555555	5554444444	8266644440
8834466666	6666666606	6644883530	4408555555	5666444444
4824444488	1144844883	6666644888	8311166666	6666666666
6666064666	6664446666	0		

The above CIAS data was compiled during a 31-minute English class.

101 (tallies in Category 8) divided by 101 (sum of tallies in Category 8 plus Category 9) = 100%.

About a third of the talk by students lasted three seconds or more in any one category: PSSR = 33 (tallies in 8-8 cell and 9-9 cell) divided by 101 (sum of tallies in Category 8 plus Category 9) = 32.67%.

This means that most of the students' responses were short, perhaps only a few words (smaller number of tallies in 8-8 cell compared with total number of tallies in Category 8).

A little over half of the instructor's talk lasted more than three seconds: TSSR = 282 (sum of the tallies of seven cells: 6 in 1-1, 2 in 2-2, 15 in 3-3, 92 in 4-4, 94 in 5-5, 73 in 6-6, 0 in 7-7) divided by 497 (total tallies in Categories 1-7) = 56.74%.

Since most college classes reveal a much higher TSSR, and because of our analysis of other key categories dealing with cues, questions, corrective/feedback, and pupil cognitive talk, we can draw an inference that the instructor was engaging the students in relatively substantial interaction compared to most other college classes.

The instructor appeared to be in control of the lesson, an inference drawn from total number of tallies in steady-state cells (PSSR, TSSR). The climate of the classroom appeared to encourage student participation (tallies in Categories 1 and 2 versus the zero number of tallies in Category 7). This was obviously a cognitive-oriented lesson (large number of tallies in Categories 3, 4, 5, 6, and 8).

Practice Makes Proficient

You need to practice with CIAS by replaying an audiotape of one of your lessons. If another instructor is interested in CIAS training, ask him/her to practice with you so you can take turns discussing each other's recorded classroom data. If the two of you disagree, discuss why and attempt to reach a consensus. This also builds a nice "support group" that can "talk about teaching." You are making excellent progress when other observers and you agree 65% or more of the time, but don't expect to reach such a lofty height during the first few hours of skill train- ing. After you have become proficient in the use of CIAS you may want to conduct research using the system; for research purposes, it would be best if observers practice until they reach an agreement level of 85% or greater.

Practice Lesson. A short lesson of about 10 minutes is located in the appendix. The goal of the lesson is to discuss various types of energy, while focusing on nuclear energy. The specific objective is to have the students identify at least four sources of energy, differentiate between fission and fusion, and identify one favorable aspect and one unfavorable aspect of fission and of fusion.

The lesson is a *real* lesson taught to *real* students, and it demonstrates how an instructor can do the following *within 10 minutes*:

- State a generic goal for the lesson in an opening statement.

- State a behavioral objective for the lesson.

- Present more than 15 facts and two major concepts.

- Ask 13 questions.

- Bring closure to this segment of the content.

7 Case Studies

Case studies are widely used in law and business courses. They are appropriate for other disciplines when the lesson objectives include analyzing, synthesizing, and judging. When using case studies, the instructor provides the students with ample background information and data about a hypothetical situation so they can attack a problem and apply basic concepts and principles.

A case is a scaled-down replication of a real experience or series of events, with ample problems or issues to generate a good discussion. You might interview people about normal, everyday happenings that include realistic confrontations, ambiguities, problems, issues, crises, and controversies. Then provide students with materials that set up specific situations and problems, followed by a series of questions.

Christensen and Hansen, *Teaching and the Case Method* (1987, p. 4), recommend the case method approach for four reasons:

- Discussion techniques, like the case study method, may be the best way to respond to course objectives that involve higher cognitive skills and affective development.

- Instructors can better analyze their ability to lead discussions by use of cases. (This would be a good reason to use CIAS with an audiotape of one of your case study sessions — to analyze your ability to handle discussions.)

- The case method approach is more relevant than many other strategies, since it brings the students closer to reality.

- The case method approach is a scholarly undertaking that "offers opportunities for systematic inquiry and rigorous reasoning."

Learned, "Reflections of a Case Method Teacher" (1987), offers several suggestions from students who participated in case studies:

- Establish a clear set of objectives for the case study.

- Provide leadership during discussions: intercede if students stray off the track,

and raise some key questions to help them refocus their efforts.

- Keep the students from continually repeating lessons already learned.

- Build on any important items that emerge as sidelines during the discussions. (I call these "teachable moments" — if they're relevant, tackle them.)

- Insist that students declare their positions.

- Stress attendance and participation.

- Cue the students when they're moving in the appropriate direction, with a comment such as "That's an interesting proposal, Jean."

- Use the opening minutes to solicit a list of key topics to be discussed.

- Encourage and guide, but refrain from actively participating.

- Give a critique in the middle and at the end of a class period.

Hansen, "Suggestions for Seminar Participants" (1987), wisely suggests that instructors encourage class participation and communication by not providing answers. If a student asks a question, turn it back to the class or choose another student to respond.

Hansen offers another suggestion: "To help sustain a smooth pace and further encourage the group to work together, you might call on two or three students at once and ask them to collaborate on some particularly elusive point of discussion for the rest of the class" (p. 59).

What is the instructor's role when using the case study method? Christensen (1987) suggests that the emphasis should be on *encouraging learning* instead of *stressing teaching*. He proposes that the instructor must move away from the "status of a center-stage, intellectually superior authority figure." The instructor must teach the skills of "observation, listening, communication, and decision-making by modeling such practices as a teacher in the classroom" (pp. 31-32).

How does the instructor prepare for day-today class sessions with case studies? Christensen suggests the following steps (pp. 38-39):

- Review objectives for the class session (usually problem-solving objectives).

- Prepare materials you will distribute for students to read.

- Consider critical issues and topics yet to be covered.

- Summarize notes following each class session, and make a general review of previous class sessions.

- Analyze the simulated industry, business or organizational situation and suggest possible solutions to problems. Then develop a set of appropriate recommendations.

- Hypothesize how the discussion of the case will progress.

- Consider the background and experiences of each student's strengths and limitations.

- Consider your attitude about the case to prevent your own biases from emerging and distorting student learning.

- Attempt to develop opening comments and closing summaries.

One of the major lessons learned by the faculty associated with developing instructional case studies for the Harvard Business School was that instructors can learn a lot about their teaching if they willingly work together to analyze what happened while teaching cases.

Simulations

Simulations are closely allied to case studies. They are particularly useful when lesson objectives include recognition of and appreciation for the values and attitudes of other groups and cultures. To set up a simulation, the instructor obtains as much information as possible about the group or culture to be studied, and students play the roles of people from that group or culture. The instructor sets the stage for the activity by establishing ground rules, providing materials, and selecting players.

There are important advantages to simulation strategies:

- They can help students gain insights into their real feelings about situations, events, people, and cultures.

- They can be fun; students are positive in their feelings about simulation strategies.

- They can motivate students to pursue information that might otherwise be of little interest to them.

- They can unleash creativity.

- They encourage spontaneity.

- They generally capture information, attitudes, and feelings in such a way that they're moved to long-term memory, a much stronger outcome than through passive learning strategies.

- They provide opportunities for students to try behaviors different from those they normally display.

- Students can better appreciate the attitudes of others: they can observe the behaviors of other students, listen to their suggestions, and build a respect for the viewpoints expressed by others.

There are some caveats:

- Simulations require very little student preparation, although the instructor should have a solid set of objectives in mind before engaging students in the use of this strategy.

- Simulation can be very time-consuming. It wouldn't be appropriate to use if the course objectives are strongly oriented to covering a multitude of facts.

- Some students may not want to express themselves during simulation strategies; their self-esteem or self-confidence might be low, and they might find the experience threatening.

- Some students give simulation very little credence. One way to overcome this negative reaction is to invite a top management administrator (vice president, chief executive officer, manager) from business, industry, or education to visit your class and talk with your students about the benefits of simulation.

- Instructors need experience in using the strategy; you would be better prepared to use it if you attended training sessions. The experience of going through simulations with role playing prior to using the strategy in your classes would help you understand simulation procedures and build your confidence.

- Participants may not have enough basic knowledge about the culture or people to make meaningful contributions.

- There is always the danger of overly aggressive students dominating the scenario; some may make fun of those who play the roles. You can prevent most of this by orienting the students to the proper behavior you expect during simulation and role playing.

What are some suggestions for first-time users of simulations?

- Prepare carefully; determine and keep in mind your objectives for the lesson.

- Take time to discuss the strategy with students prior to their first experience with role playing and simulation.

- Be sure to explain to the students how the activity relates to the lesson and course objectives.

- Develop a wholesome classroom climate prior to implementing the strategy. I wait several weeks in my courses before using simulation and role playing.

- Try to list the questions you hope students will raise when they discuss the simulation; interject those that are not produced by the students.

- Involve as many students as possible. You may want to have the same situation replayed by three different groups of students.

Field Trips

Sometimes an instructor may prefer to take the students away from the campus to observe some phenomenon. Settings for field trips are quite diverse: the court house, a local business, an art museum, an industrial site, a funeral parlor, a historical location, a farm or ranch, multiple sites where oil rigs are located, a statesman's home, and so forth. Some trips are relatively simple; others can be quite ambitious.

First you need to decide if the field trip is the best way for students to accomplish the objective(s) for your proposed lesson. If a field trip seems appropriate to your objective(s), you need to check your institution's faculty/student handbooks for answers to questions involving pertinent regulations, including:

- Clear everything with your immediate supervisor, usually the department chair.

- Obtain permission slips.

- Check on insurance.

- Arrange for transportation.

- Check out admission fees.

- Complete official forms, either by the students or you in advance.

- Note any reports to be filed after the trip.

Next, organize the field trip. A few guiding questions:

- When will the trip take place?

- Where will students meet?

- How will students travel to the site?

- How will money be collected?

- What arrangements must be made for meals or overnight accommodations?

- What medical supplies may be needed?

- Whom should you contact in case of an emergency?

You also need to prepare a handout for the students indicating the purpose of the trip and your objectives, with a guide sheet, map, and departure/arrival times.

You still have some important tasks to complete prior to the day of the field trip. Personally go over the details with officials at the site — time, date, number of students, person to contact on arrival, etc. Ask them about safety precautions and other restrictions they might have. For example, chemicals in a building may prevent travel by students with contact lenses, or you might discover the site isn't accessible to handicapped students.

One of the more important tasks is for you to take the field trip yourself *before* taking your students. You may discover that the trip takes longer than you estimated, so you would change your departure and return times. You may discover that a site or building is extremely hot or cold, so you should recommend that your students dress appropriately. You might discover a very interesting phenomenon at the site that students should note when they take the trip. You will also want to obtain the names of key personnel at the site so you can add them to your handouts. This personal visit also provides you with the opportunity to discuss with on-site personnel your purpose and objectives, as well as any items you'd like them to emphasize during the trip. An advance visit also allows you to better prepare your students, with confidence and authority.

Finally, consider follow-up discussion and

activities. Is the discussion best handled at the site, after departing from the site, or in the next class session? What is an appropriate and meaningful follow-up activity — oral reports, term papers, tests?

Many beginning instructors avoid field trips. Others dread the preparation and supervision, or may question the "pedagogical justification" of such trips. Others simply feel uncomfortable about taking out a group of students as if they were a fourth-grade class. But if a field trip is appropriate to your objectives, and if you plan properly, it can be an effective and satisfying strategy/activity.

Keller Plan

A Keller Plan divides the course into sections or units of study. Students refer to printed guides to help them progress through the course at their own pace. Of course, the instructor or an assistant is available to help those students who need extra coaching or who have questions for which answers are not found in the guides and instructional materials. If the course is linear, you can establish unit tests and require students to reach an acceptable level of mastery prior to moving into the next unit of study. This means that some students may have to recycle through the materials and activities for a unit until they meet the predetermined "pass and progress" level, a kind of prerequisite before moving into the next section of study.

A Keller Plan has five features that set it apart from traditional instructional strategies:

1) The Keller Plan is mastery-oriented, with a heavy emphasis on 2) individual pacing and 3) self-tutoring. You have to determine in advance what you'll accept as "mastery" of the unit and how you'll measure the progress of the students to see if they have reached your mastery level requirements.

One fall term, I visited a college where a Keller Plan was in operation for students in Chemistry I and Chemistry II. I noted two students seated in study carrels side by side; one student was completing Chemistry II while the other was halfway through Chemistry I. However, the first student had been at the college only a few months, while the second student was completing her second year. The second student had been receiving "Incomplete" on her semester grade sheets because she was still struggling to learn the basic knowledge required to "pass and progress" through the units and into Chemistry

II. The first student was extremely bright, entered with excellent prerequisites, sailed through Chemistry I, and was moving swiftly through Chemistry II. These two students illustrate the advantages of the Keller Plan.

4) The Keller Plan uses printed study guides to communicate information. You need to invest a lot of time into developing these study guides. The units should include introductions, objectives, cues, content, activities, directions, and self-scoring progress tests with feedback, so the students can tell if they are ready to take the unit test in an attempt to "pass and progress" into the next unit. I also recommend that you have a few students with diverse backgrounds read your study guides before you use them; students can provide excellent feedback about the study guides, e.g., "I didn't understand this section at all" or "This chart didn't seem to be very useful."

5) The Keller Plan includes a few lectures by the instructor to motivate students. You could post a notice on the bulletin board or write directly to the students to communicate the times, dates, locations, titles, and content of various lectures.

Instructors are interested in providing more opportunities for students to move at their own learning pace, and the Keller Plan is an illustration of how that concern can be addressed.

Laboratory Method

This method is widely used in scientific settings. The students can observe phenomena and the operation of substances, e.g., observing what happens when two specific chemicals are mixed. Students enrolled in art courses always find that studio laboratories accompany their painting or sculpturing activities. Architecture courses provide laboratory opportunities for students to build small-scale replications of much larger buildings or bridges. The laboratory method is appropriate for objectives which deal with research methods, application, and observation skills.

Laboratory instruction is one of the more practical alternatives to the lecture. It takes students away from the theoretical setting of the textbook and lecture, to confront them with problems to solve, experiments to conduct, demonstrations to observe, exercises to complete, short-term and long-term projects to pursue, or data to collect so they can interpret and draw conclusions. The focus is on having students instruct themselves and teach their peers.

Brown and Atkins, *Effective Teaching* (1988, p. 91), identify the following as worthwhile goals for laboratory teaching:

- Instructing students in manual and observational skills germane to the content of the lesson.

- Developing knowledge of the scientific method.

- Providing an opportunity to apply the scientific method to solving problems.

- Creating a mentorship setting that might nurture professional attitudes.

Brown and Atkins emphasize that students must view laboratory tasks as meaningful and pertinent. I recall an excellent laboratory experience, a semester project in architecture that took students through a series of activities, including short lectures, studio activities, and a field project, exemplifying the true meaning of laboratory teaching and practical implementation. The instructor challenged students to use what they had learned from his lectures by observing the downtown area of the city, where several buildings were empty and owners of other stores were considering leaving because of the popularity of the large shopping malls. The students sketched new storefronts that might appeal more to would-be shoppers. Next, the students actually compiled a small newspaper about downtown shopping, with their sketches of the storefronts, and distributed copies to the merchants and friends. Soon some of the merchants invested in new storefronts. The spruced-up downtown area began to draw residents back for dining and shopping. I can't think of a better application of laboratory teaching — relevant, meaningful, practical.

The instructor must develop good communication and organization skills when using the laboratory method. Students must understand the goals and purposes of the laboratory lessons, or chances of successful laboratory experiences will be diminished.

Research assistants and teaching assistants should feel at home in laboratory settings. It's useful for the instructor to spend time with the assistants in preparing the lab experiences. Instructors should discuss difficulties the assistants might encounter, help them prepare questions, and provide ideas for helping slower students during lessons. In preparing the assistants, the instructor also indirectly communicates to the assistant that laboratory experiences are important for the students. These interactions between instructor and graduate assistant represent a type of mentoring — adequately preparing future professors for tomorrow's classrooms.

8 Term Papers and Oral Reports

Barratt, "Ten Things That Teachers Should Teach (and Students Should Learn) About Language" (1988), pleads for instructors to give more attention to formal writing and speaking and how they relate directly to students' personal environment. Writing papers and giving oral reports provide golden opportunities to build on the following points that Barratt believes everyone should learn (pp. 70-71):

- Language is legitimate.
- Other people's language is legitimate.
- Formal writing and formal speaking call for conventions different from those involved in informal uses.
- Formal features of English are arbitrary.
- Languages change.
- Lack of knowledge and lack of formal language conventions are not the same.
- Grammar can be developed at any time in any setting.
- Language can be interesting.

Term Papers

Many instructors assign term papers. In fact, they're so much a part of higher education that they need little comment here. But perhaps they're so important for some wrong reasons: some instructors feel that they're simply the "right way" to arrive at a grade for the students, while some students believe that instructors like term papers because they're easier to assign. So it may be worthwhile to recall several basic advantages of this traditional activity:

- Students increase their knowledge of the topic.
- Students learn how to use library and human resources.
- Students benefit from applying higher cognitive processes.
- Students learn how to organize their thoughts for others.

From Term Papers to Oral Reports

Instructors can promote additional benefits by requiring oral reports about the term papers. A five-minute oral report on the salient parts of a paper provides an opportunity for the student to practice the art of summarization and speaking skills. The student can also learn to direct discussions if the instructor adds a question-and-answer session at the end of the report.

I observed an excellent use of this strategy in a construction management course that emphasized legal aspects from a lawyer's point of view. Each student was assigned a topic to pursue in depth during the semester and to apply what he/she learned to a fictitious company created by the instructor. Near the end of the term, the instructor invited some colleagues to attend the class and role play the president, vice president, comptroller, and board members for the fictitious company.

Each student would make a five-minute oral presentation about some legal aspect covered in the course, but within the context of the fictitious company. For example, one student was very interested in the legal aspects of union and non-union contracts. In his presentation he recommended that the instructor's colleagues contract with unionized labor for a construction project. The instructor's colleagues then simulated their roles and asked the student penetrating questions, such as "What would happen if we hired a non-union group just to install the electricity and plumbing in the new building?" The student had to provide reasons to support his original recommendation, and he could reference studies that involved real legal battles that had taken place in similar situations. It was an excellent experience for the students.

Term papers represent still another way that instructors can capitalize on strategies that recognize differences among students. A student may wish to pursue a particular topic in more depth, and the flexibility of the term paper provides an opportunity for the instructor to capitalize on that individual's high intrinsic motivation to seek more information about the topic.

Media and Materials

We have a vast array of media and materials to support our instructional efforts. I shall discuss those types that I believe a beginning instructor is most likely to encounter: multimedia, audio-tutorial, blackboard, and microcomputers.

Multi-Media Techniques

Sometimes the objectives for a lesson can best be reached by using videotaped programs, films, color slides, transparencies, radio programs, or telephone conversations. Of course, the objectives should always determine the choice of media, not the reverse.

An oceanography instructor carried a high-powered microscope and video camera to the Gulf of Mexico one summer so she could videotape organisms in their actual environment. She now replays those tapes in her oceanography course whenever she wants her students to study the Gulf of Mexico organisms.

A philosophy instructor uses movies such as *Dead Poets Society* and *Grapes of Wrath* as motivational introductions to selected topics in his values course.

An instructor in soil and crop sciences uses 2" x 2" color slides made from photographs of various grains so he can project pictures of the grains on a screen that everyone in the classroom can observe simultaneously.

Color transparencies have become popular with many instructors. You could make a transparency of a chart, map, graph, photograph, etc. from a source other than the basic textbook and project it on a large screen during a lecture.

A speech instructor likes to use audiotapes of old radio programs to highlight communication skills that enable listeners to conjure up their own images of scenes portrayed during broadcasts.

A building and construction instructor enjoys arranging for a telephone conversation with an adjunct professor at a university in another state.

The whole arena of multi-media is vast, a broad topic that this book can't begin to cover. However, I would encourage you to either purchase a multi-media instructional textbook or go to the library and check out such a book to read and study.

For more in-depth coverage of the use of media in teaching, you may want to review Craig N. Locatis and Francis D. Atkinson, *Media and Technology for Education and Training* (1984). Locatis and Atkinson focus their textbook on using media for teaching at all levels of education. They present their chapters in three parts: Part I consists of media, applications, instructional development, and selecting instructional media; Part I covers print media, graphic and object media, photographic media, audio media, TV and video, computers, and simulations and games; Part III deals with instructional design, principles of use, evaluation, and what the authors foresee in the future.

Audio-Tutorial Programs

Postlethwait, *The Audio-Tutorial Approach to Learning: Through Independent Study and Integrated Experiences* (1969), developed one of the more successful programs that recognizes and accommodates differences in students' rates of learning. It combined a variety of approaches that enabled his biology students to use multiple senses to better learn course material. This is what Postlethwait does:

- He provides a handbook to accompany the program.

- He provides audio tapes, slides, and other media to accompany the lessons in his handbook.

- He provides a weekly motivational lecture or invites a guest speaker to start that week's unit of study.

- He arranges for space and resources for students to conduct experiments on an individual basis, if the lesson calls for experimentation.

- He requires students to progress through a weekly lesson at each student's own speed within an open laboratory setting where materials and tutors are available.

The Blackboard as Media

One of the best resources we have in our classrooms is the blackboard. Most classrooms have blackboards (sometimes greenboards or whiteboards) with chalk or colored markers and erasers.

Sounds simple enough, doesn't it? However, sometimes we're not as thoughtful as we should be when using the board.

Organization is an important aspect of

boardsmanship. There should be a logical flow of information as we write items on the blackboard.

Answer the following questions before you write on the board:

- What do I want my students to know at the end of the lesson?

- What should I select to put on the board?

- How should I organize my statements so they have some logic and reason for being highlighted on the board?

- When should I put the materials on the board? When should I erase them?

A few more guidelines when using the board:

- Don't stand in front of your writing when lecturing. Step aside so the students can see what you are referencing when discussing items on the board.

- Don't be too quick to erase what you've written on the board. Remember: it takes students more time to logically organize and to process the information we put on the board than it takes us to fill the board with our words of wisdom. Erase only the oldest information, after you're sure the students have had ample time to copy it.

- Don't pack the board with too much information. The key is to include only *important* information. And determine in advance the "board life" of your material: some items you may need for only a few minutes, while others should remain on the board for the entire class session.

- Be the student. Walk to the back of the room and sit in the seat farthest from the board. Make sure you write or print large enough for the students to see from the back of the room. Are there any intervening obstacles, such as an overhead projector, lectern, boxes on tables, etc. that might prevent the students from seeing what's on the board?

- Write legibly; if your writing is terrible, print. Students won't benefit from our preparation if they can't interpret what we write. Be careful to write out the whole word instead of using shorthand tricks to save time. Students often write only the shortened forms — which they may no longer understand when they review their notes.

- Try to visualize the space you'll need on the board, or sketch on paper the items you want to put on the board, so you have some idea about how much space they will take. Remember that students are generally taking notes on vertical, 8 1/2" x 11" sheets of paper, while you are using a horizontal board of quite different dimensions.

- Some instructors will enter the classroom ahead of schedule and lightly outline any sketches they are going to make during a lesson. Then when they arrive at the point in the lecture when they need the sketch, they can draw heavily over the light outline or perhaps use colored chalk to highlight the sketch.

- Avoid unnecessary competition. Sometimes what you put on the board may distract students from what you're saying five minutes later.

Microcomputers

What an impact the microcomputer has had on business, government, and educational settings! It seems that today's graduates *must* know how to use microcomputers and programs because more courses are being developed that incorporate teaching through computers.

The microcomputer is transforming the world: we're using them in ever-increasing ways in business, industry, government, and our homes. There are exciting possibilities in education as well, and instructors in the '90s should make the most of our computer opportunities. Computer programs:

- Can improve study skills.

- Can "tutor" many students at their own pace through well-designed problem-solving activities.

- Can simulate experiences from the world of work.

Instructors at Texas A&M University have used incentive grants from the university's Center for Teaching Excellence to assist them in developing some very innovative microcomputer programs. They report that the time involved in developing microcomputer programs is well worth the effort.

What are the possibilities in the college setting? Here are some:

- A rule-based, computer-aided design package could assist in the design of wood structures.

- A series of interactive question-and-answer sessions could quiz students in cellular physiology and neurophysiology.

- A data base for general pathology could allow medical students to select a body part on the screen and progressively focus in on that part of the body, just as they would increase the power of a microscope.

- Self-instructional programs can provide immediate feedback and reinforcement to students in chemistry labs.

- Computerized case studies in clinical chemistry can enrich and supplement the existing curriculum.

- Testing programs, simulations, and word games can greatly enhance classroom experiences in foreign languages.

- Computer applications can be used in teaching writing and literature. Marcus, "Compupoem: A Computer-Assisted Writing Activity" (1982), provided an example of a computer program for writing poetry. Selfe, "Software for Hardness: CAI for College Composition Teachers" (1984), used a computer-assisted instruction program in first-year English composition classes. The program consisted of eight writing assignments involving description, narration, personal writing, classification, evaluation, persuasion, comparison-contrast, and literary analysis.

- Programs can be used with nursing students to develop their ability to calculate medication dosages.

- Programs can be used to implement practical experience in solving simple business problems.

- Programs can present steps in the diagnostic reasoning process, recognition of relevant and irrelevant cues, and linking cues to clinical situations for students.

- Programs can be used in physics classes to help students develop the scientific method approach in solving problems.

- Instructors in biology can use computers to teach students how to collect, retrieve, and analyze information, and then have the students draw conclusions.

An easy-to-read 1989 Phi Delta Kappa Educational Foundation Fastback also provides an excellent overview of uses of the computer with video. It may provide you with additional insight into the rapidly expanding use of computers in today's educational setting (see Beardslee and Davis, *Interactive Videodisc and the Teaching-Learning Process,* 1989).

The following are other references you may want to review:

William G. Camp, *Microcomputer Applications for Students of Agriculture,* 1988; Steven Gordon and Richard F. Anderson, *Microcomputer Applications in City Planning and Management,* 1989; Robert T. Grauer and Paul K. Sugrue, *Microcomputer Applications,* 1989; David H. Jonassen (editor), *Instructional Designs for Microcomputer Courseware,* 1988; Donald D. Spencer and Susan L. Spencer, *Drawing with a Microcomputer,* 1989; Ali Galip Ulsoy and Warren R. DeVries, *Microcomputer Applications in Manufacturing,* 1989.

9   Testing and Evaluating Students

Testing is a common task confronting instructors, but it shouldn't be taken lightly. Tests serve three major purposes:

- They provide a record of data so the instructor can give students grades.

- They provide a learning experience for the students: the results enable them to correct their misunderstandings or to seek help from the instructor.

- They motivate students. Anytime I announced that there would be a test on Friday covering the first three chapters of the basic text, students read and reviewed those chapters " some for the first time.

Prerequisite Testing

A number of instructors administer prerequisite assessment tests during the first week of classes. This form of testing serves an important purpose in determining if the students enrolled in the course have the prerequisite knowledge to succeed in the program. First, the instructor develops a set of objectives for the course, listing what he/she wants the students to be able to do when they complete the course. Next the instructor determines which prerequisites will be required for the students to complete the course successfully, then develops a diagnostic test to measure those prerequisite skills and knowledge.

For example, prerequisite knowledge about polynomial arithmetic may be required before the student can master a specific objective for the course. Therefore, the prerequisite test needs to include diagnostic items on exponents, combining similar terms, the distributive property, binomials, simplifying polynomials, and division of polynomials. If the student can't handle those items, the instructor should advise him/her to enroll in a prerequisite course, although some students may be able to continue in a course if they have difficulty only with division of polynomials.

Tell the students why you are administering the prerequisite test and inform them that it doesn't count for a grade.

Testing During the Second Week

Another approach you might consider is to develop a battery of test items over course content, based on your original set of objectives. Then, the second week of the course, you could administer the battery of items to the students, informing them that the test doesn't count for a grade, although students who reach your predetermined success level could receive credit. This type of test serves the following purposes:

1) If a student has the prerequisite knowledge and skills and has already reached your predetermined success level for the course, you could arrange for independent enrichment activities, rather than bore him/her with information that he/she has mastered already. Or you could advise him/her to drop your course and take a more advanced course.

2) If the course is organized as a self-instructional program arranged around weekly units of study, analysis of the data could assist you in placing the student in the appropriate self-instructional module. For example, if you have 16 modules organized in a linear manner, your analysis may lead you to conclude that one student could skip the first seven modules and begin with the eighth, while a second student may have to begin with the first or second module.

3) If your course is organized as lectures and your analysis reveals that a majority of the students are strong in some areas of content but weak in others, you may emphasize the content where the data indicate the students are weak. You could bypass or touch lightly on content that students already appear to know.

Testing During the Course

You may want to administer quizzes throughout the entire semester to determine if the students are progressing toward completion of the objectives and to identify problems the students may be having in the course. Quizzes may reveal a need to backtrack and review material with additional examples and illustrations. Through periodic quizzes, instructors can identify the students who would benefit from corrective measures before they fall too far behind in the course.

I believe quizzes and grades provide external motivation for some students. Moreover, they can be powerful learning experiences if the test situation provides opportunities for students to recall information, reorganize thoughts, and use higher cognitive processes. Therefore, frequent testing can help students reinforce what they have learned: if the tests are good, preparing for them requires the students to rethink what they've studied.

Testing at the End of the Course

If the students pass the final exam, they should feel comfortable moving into the next module or course of study because they know they have the required prerequisite knowledge and skills to succeed.

However, analysis of final examination data may lead you to revise your course if large numbers of students are not reaching acceptable levels of success. If they are typical students, and no extenuating reasons can be detected for their failure to achieve, then you should review your materials, procedures, learning activities, instructional strategies, and attitude to see if changes may be necessary.

Norm-Referenced Testing

Norm-referenced testing involves a relative system for evaluating and grading students in relation to their peers. An individual's effort from one test to another is *not* considered in this type of testing, because the test is designed to discriminate among those enrolled in the course. Grades are usually assigned on the basis of the normal curve, which assumes the achievement of the students is normally distributed.

There are some limitations surrounding norm-referenced testing:

1) Two sections of the same course may be divided in such a way that more of the brighter, more knowledgeable students are enrolled in one section. Use of norms will penalize a number of bright, knowledgeable students in the first section because there are more comparable students in that section. More of the less knowledgeable, less bright students in the second section will receive higher scores than those with the same knowledge and brightness if they were in the first section.

2) Scores alone do not communicate the level of knowledge and skills obtained by the students in the course. Students become the reference point, not their knowledge of content or their level of performance skills. If 70 is the highest score on the examination, the normal curve converts the score to an A — unless the instructor sets minimums such as "no A's for scores under 90 and no B's for scores under 80."

Criterion-Referenced Testing

To avoid the above limitations of norm-referenced testing, some instructors have implemented criterion-referenced testing. Criterion-referenced testing involves a predetermined set of performance statements which students pursue without relation to peer progress. Criterion-referenced tests use predetermined standards for grading. Therefore, the achievement statement must be quite precise since the instructor does not assign *certain percentages* of A's, B's, C's, D's and F's to the class of students. All students could receive an A on an examination if they reached the predetermined set of performance statements.

Examples of criterion-referenced statements would be: the student will identify all three branches of government or the student will run a 100-meter dash in less than 12 seconds. If the student responds correctly, the student receives 100% or A on that part of the examination. This process continues throughout the entire examination. Credit is given for reaching the predetermined acceptable performance level.

Criterion-referenced testing also has limitations:

1) As mentioned above, all the students could receive A's on the test or for the course. This drives some registrars, administrators, and faculty crazy because they are accustomed to a spread in grades, a *discrimination* among students in the course. They don't understand or accept criterion-based approaches to evaluation, although business has used such assessment for decades — either a salesperson sells $300,000 in computers during the year or he/she is fired; either the widget meets a predetermined specification or it isn't released from the assembly line; either the hamburgers are purchased within X number of minutes after cooking or they're discarded.

2) Since criterion-referenced testing doesn't require discrimination among students,

prospective employers or graduate schools have no way of knowing how the students compare with their counterparts.

3) Some students who could finish a course by getting D's on norm-referenced tests may not complete a criterion-referenced course because they fail to meet a predetermined mastery level on the tests. Some instructors give such students a grade of "incomplete" and require them to retake the course or the module until they reach the acceptable level of performance.

Criterion-referenced tests appear to go well with mastery-learning programs, since they have absolute standards for acceptable performance.

There are a number of different types of tests and evaluation procedures. In the following section I will discuss essay tests, completion tests, matching tests, true/false tests, and multiple-choice tests.

Essay Tests

Essay tests are well-suited for assessing the ability to use higher cognitive processes because they provide students with an opportunity to use interpretations and generalizations. Instructors need to consider several factors when using essay tests. They need to announce in advance the criteria they will use to grade students' responses. The criteria may include:

- good writing
- correct spelling
- legibility
- coherence
- relevance (dealing only with the topic)

The criteria should be discussed with students before they prepare for the examination so they understand the grading procedures and have a better idea of how to prepare for the test.

When the essay test consists of more than one question, students should be required to respond to all of the items. This provides a common reference point for the instructor. If students are allowed to "select two of the three questions," the instructor may make inaccurate assumptions. For example, Sally may have been versed on all three items, but Jean may not know anything about question number two because she failed to prepare for that question's content. Yet, the instructor might erroneously conclude from their written responses that Sally and Jean had equal competence if they have the right to select two of the three items.

Essay tests may be easier to develop than good objective types of tests, but essay tests are more difficult to grade and may be more time-consuming to score. One must also consider reliability in grading. Some classic studies have revealed that professors from the same discipline assigned grades ranging from A to F on identical essay responses; a typed list of criteria placed alongside the student's paper for reference during the grading helps prevent some of the problems cited earlier.

Also, before grading essays, fold each student's name under, to hide it while you're reading the paper: this helps prevent "halo" influences. If you see Sally's name on the paper, you might give it a higher score than it deserves simply because Sally is a very bright student who agrees with you during class. Or a paper with Mike's name might get a better grade simply because Mike always smiles in class. No, this technique isn't foolproof. You might begin to recognize the handwriting of students as the course progresses through the semester; however, it's worth considering.

If you want to go all out against "halo" influences, ask the students to use pseudonyms:

1. On the first day, ask each student to create a pseudonym, then to write or type the pseudonym and his/her real name on a 3" x 5" index card.

2. The students turn in their cards. You place the cards in an envelope, seal it, then set it aside until you've recorded the final grades.

3. Each student turns in another 3" x 5" card with just his/her pseudonym. Use these cards to list names (pseudonyms) in your grade book.

4. Students use their pseudonyms on all tests and written assignments.

5. You score the tests or assignments and record the grades in your grade book. At the close of the next class session, you set the papers out on your table or desk, then depart *before* the students retrieve them.

6. At the close of the course, when you've recorded all the grades, you open the sealed envelope and match final grades with the real names.

Of course, it may not be possible for you to use pseudonyms in your course because you want to meet each student personally or you want each student to feel free to conference with you about any test or assignment (or you include oral exercises or class participation in their grades).

The following are examples of essay questions:

- List and discuss what you consider to be three major reasons for the North defeating the South during the Civil War. Support your answers by referencing primary and secondary sources.

- Compare and contrast three top generals for the South with three top generals for the North.

- Discuss three reasons for supporting wildlife conservation. Support your reasons.

- Explain why it is important for building construction students to know and understand the legal aspects involved in a contract to build a government building.

When grading essay exams, most authorities on testing recommend reading all of the students' responses to the first question before proceeding to the students' responses to the second question. They also recommend two readings of the responses to each question.

After the first reading of the responses to the first question, while referencing your list of criteria, sort the papers into five stacks, putting the best essays in the first stack and the poorest essays in the fifth stack. Put the others in the middle three stacks, setting those that are closer to the best in the second stack and those that are closer to the poorest in the fourth stack. Now you will have five common reference points.

Then read all essays a second time and make any suitable adjustments of the papers: on a second reading, an essay may appear better or worse than judged at first and you may decide to move it to another stack. Eventually, you assign grades to the essays. You could assign A's to stack one, B's to stack two, C's to stack three, D's to stack four, and F's to stack five. If you believe all of the papers in stacks four and five deserve the higher grade, give them all D's. This is where subjective grading takes place, as you assign the grades you believe are appropriate for the first essay in relation to others in the same stack.

Next, read all responses to the second essay question following the procedure described above. Finally, you will have to assign an overall grade for each student's total number of responses.

Completion Tests

Sentence-completion tests, sometimes called short-answer tests, ask students to use a word or phrase to complete a statement. Be very careful when constructing sentence-completion tests. When the students read the sentence, they should have no difficulty understanding what response you are seeking. To help eliminate ambiguity, have a few colleagues and/or former students read an item, then ask them for their reactions: "Did you have difficulty understanding any part of the sentence? Did you know the answer I was seeking? What was it?"

Another recommendation is to place the fill-in space in a location other than as the first or last words of the statement. The closer to the middle, the better " but not at the risk of coherence. This recommendation enables the student to take full advantage of contextual cues.

Completion tests are particularly valuable if you want the students to move from recall of exact words to the next higher level of the cognitive domain, comprehension. The test can require students to use their own words from what they've learned.

You can establish grade points for each correct response. Difficult items geared to very important objectives might be worth five points per item, while items for less important objectives may be worth one point each. The point value for each item should be identified on the test; the directions might indicate that the first 15 items have a value of five points each, while the remaining 25 items have a value of one point each, for a grand total of 100 points.

The following are examples of completion items:

- President John F. Kennedy approved the Bay of Pigs invasion, during which _____ made up the main forces landing on the beaches of Cuba.

- During Lyndon B. Johnson's first campaign for the U.S. Senate, _____ served as his advisor, close associate, and campaign manager.

Be sure you provide enough space for students to respond, and make all of the completion lines of equal length.

Matching Items Tests

A matching items test consists of two related lists of words, symbols, pictures, or statements. Matching tests are very useful when you've emphasized dates, events, locations, treaties, and persons: you can quickly and effectively measure the ability of the students to recall and match such items.

Items in the first column (located on the left) are known as the *list of premises*. Items in the second column (located on the right) are known as the *list of responses* from which to select the match.

A few recommendations:

- Keep the items in each list homogeneous (all names, all dates, all numbers, all places, and so forth).

- Make sure there's only one correct response for each item to be matched.

- Put all options in both columns on the same page, so students don't flip pages back and forth.

- If names make up a list, list them in alphabetical order, last name first (e.g., Roosevelt, Franklin D.), so students can locate those they are attempting to match with items in the response column.

- If dates or numbers make up a list, place them in either descending or ascending order: don't jumble them.

- Make the response column (the second column) longer than the list of premises, e.g., by adding five items or so that would *not* be used, to prevent matching by a process of elimination.

The following are examples of matching tests:

1. Match the president's name in the first column with the dates of office in the second column by writing the number of the matching item on the line to the left of each president's name:

_____	Adams, John	1.	1789-1797
_____	Buchanan, James	2.	1797-1801
_____	Fillmore, Millard	3.	1807-1809
_____	Jackson, Andrew	4.	1809-1817
_____	Madison, James	5.	1817-1825
_____	Monroe, James	6.	1825-1829
_____	Pierce, Franklin	7.	1829-1837
_____	Polk, James K.	8.	1837-1841
_____	Tyler, John	9.	1841-1845
_____	Van Buren, Martin	10.	1845-1849
		11.	1849-1850
		12.	1850-1853
		13.	1853-1857
		14.	1857-1861
		15.	1861-1865

2. Match the descriptions of the treaties, agreements, and organizations in the left column with the abbreviated titles (all caps) in the right column by writing the number of the matching item on the line to the left of each description:

_____	Thailand, Malaysia, Singapore, Indonesia, and the Philippines formed this non-military alliance in 1967.	1.	EFTA
_____	This defense shield on the northern tier of the Middle East was formed in 1955 to protect against a Soviet penetration.	2.	SOA
		3.	CENTO
		4.	AEASN
_____	Organized in 1959, it was established to generate economic growth and equitable competition (Austria, Iceland, Norway, Portugal, Sweden, Switzerland, and Finland).	5.	OTNA
		6.	TFAE
		7.	OAS
_____	In 1949, this powerful organization was formed as a regional defense for the North Atlantic area.	8.	CNOTE
		9.	ASEAN
		10.	NATO
_____	Most of the countries in North, Central, and South America created this organization in 1948.		

True/False Tests

True/false tests are advantageous when objectives for the course involve knowledge and comprehension of a very large number of facts. Another advantage is the ease in scoring. In fact, a secretary or assistant could grade a true/false test for you.

A major disadvantage is that students have a 50-50 chance of guessing the correct responses. Another limitation in developing a good true/false exam is the difficulty in abolishing ambiguity. Try not to use the following words: never, always, usually, sometimes, all, only, generally, frequently.

Other recommendations for true/false tests:

- Make the length of both "true" and "false" statements similar.

- Identify an equal number of "true" items and "false" items.

- Use your own words in the test items, not the same as in the textbook.

- Refrain from using double negatives or tricky wording.

- Underline negatives used in the items.

- Randomize the order of the items, so a pattern doesn't emerge (e.g., 10 "true" followed by 10 "false," followed by 10 more "true").

The following is an example of a true/false item:

Directions. Circle T if the statement is more true than false; circle F if the statement is more false than true.

- T F Dwight D. Eisenhower served as president of the United States from 1953 into 1961.

Multiple-Choice Tests

Multiple-choice tests are flexible and can be used to test students over a large body of information. Most are either four-option or five-option, although the specific content often dictates the potential number of choices you can use. The following is an example of a multiple-choice test item:

The first president of the United States was:
a. Thomas Jefferson
b. John Quincy Adams
c. George Washington
d. None of the above.

Keep a record of your test items from semester to semester. Place each multiple-choice test item on a separate 4" x 6" index card. On the reverse side of the card, place certain data you may wish for reference purposes, e.g., the correct response, the date the item was used on a test, the number of students taking the test, and the number who answered the item correctly.

Let's study the example again. The main section (the "stem") spells out the task. After reading the stem, the student should know what to do before reading the choices (the "options"). Only one option should be the correct response. The other options (the "distractors") should be homogeneous, i.e., they should have promise as possible answers. *Don't* ask the student to identify the 16th president of the United States, and then list as the distractors such names as Marilyn Monroe, Henry Ford, and Ben Franklin. You should list as choices four presidents who served between 1830 and 1864.

The stem should:

- be brief and yet complete;

- reflect only one main idea;

- form a grammatical unit with each of the options;

- not give away the correct answer, e.g., it shouldn't call for an answer in the plural while three of the options are singular and only one option is plural.

Test Construction

You use your objectives for the course to guide you in analyzing the test. Your objectives serve as the foundation from which you develop your tests. Once you've written your objectives, you decide how much to stress each objective during the course. Give a weight to the value of each objective. For example, if you have four objectives, you might feel that the first objective is worth twice as much as any other of the remaining three objectives; give it 40% of the test emphasis, with a 20% emphasis for each of the remaining three objectives.

Validity, reliability, and practicality are additional factors to consider when constructing your tests.

Validity. This refers to the degree to which the test measures what it is purported to measure.

The following are a few ways to check the validity of evaluation instruments:

1) Cross-reference the items with textbooks, journals, and research reports to see if the items stress basic, current material.

2) Discuss the items with colleagues; ask them if they think the items are important in evaluating students.

3) If feasible, ask professionals in the discipline — former students and prospective employers — if mastery of the items is important for success in the field.

Reliability. This refers to the consistency and accuracy of student responses to test items each time the test is administered. In other words, the student's response to a test item should be basically the same if he/she completed the test today and again tomorrow without intervening variables such as learning, forgetting, illness, or emotional upset.

Reliability can be checked by using alternate forms of the same instrument, particularly if you teach multiple sections of the same course. You want *consistency* " the same results or basic agreement among the different sections. Students in section one could complete form A of the test, while students in section two could complete form B. On the second administration, section one would complete form B, while section two would complete form A. Simple correlation coefficient statistics can be used to demonstrate similarity in the results from two different administrations of the same test to the same students (called "test-retest method").

Practicality. This refers to compiling, administering, scoring, time, and cost factors. Can the evaluation instrument be developed, administered, and scored within the limitations of time and resource constraints?

Check practicality by answering the following questions:

- Which type of test will efficiently measure student progress toward the objectives in a valid, reliable way?

- Do I have the time and resources to develop and to grade this particular type of test?

- Do the students have time to complete the test?

Test Item Analysis

Test items should be analyzed to determine if they are positive or negative discriminators. If more students with high overall test scores marked an item *incorrectly* than those with low overall test scores, the item had *negative discrimination* — it's open to question. If more students with high overall test scores marked an item *correctly* than those with low overall test scores, the item had *positive discrimination*. Build a file of *positive discriminating* items, and use them in future tests. Either revise or discard *negative discriminating* items.

The following is a simple method for determining positive or negative discrimination and index difficulty — "easiness of the item" — i.e., how difficult is the item for the average student in your course?

1. Identify the 10 papers with the highest overall test scores, followed by the 10 papers with the lowest overall test scores.

2. Prepare an item analysis sheet as follows:

Item #	H	L	L+H	H-L	Comment
1					
2					
3					
4					
.					
.					
50					

The column headings of the items analysis sheet are interpreted as follows:

H = number of 10 highest-scoring students answering the test item correctly.

L = number of 10 lowest-scoring students answering the test item correctly.

H+L = number from both high and low groups answering the test item correctly.

H-L = number of high-scoring students minus the number of low-scoring students answering the test item correctly.

If the H-L column is *minus*, it indicates a *negative* discrimination: the item needs revision. If the H-L column is *plus*, it indicates *positive* discrimination.

Let's assume that on test item number one, all 10 of the highest-scoring students selected the correct response, while six of the lowest-scoring students did. Our item analysis would appear as follows:

Item #	H	L	H+L	H-L	Comment
1	10	6	16	+4	positive

Some instructors believe an index difficulty between 7 and 17 is desirable for the H+L column and an index of +3 or above for the H-L column. Personally, I've used test items with a zero index for the H-L column and an index difficulty between 18 and 20 for the H+L column. If such an item reinforces learning and rewards students, I am in favor of keeping it for future tests.

You should also check test *reliability*. A quick and easy way is to use a scattergram (examples appear in Figures 5-7) based on split halves of an entire test:

1. Divide the test into two parts, with even-numbered items (2, 4, 6, 8 ... 100) representing one half of the test and odd-numbered items (1, 3, 5, 7 ... 99) representing the other half of the test. This is preferable to using items one through 50 as part one and items 51 through 100 as part two, since all students may not complete the final items, or they may become fatigued near the end of the exam.

2. Design a scattergram like the one displayed in Figure 6 (page 60).

Look at student number one's score for the first test half (in my earlier example, the odd-numbered items 1, 3, 5 etc. through 99) and his score for the second test half (in my earlier example, the even-numbered items 2, 4, 6 etc. through 100). Place a dot where his two scores intersect on the scattergram. If he had 50 correct on the first half and 48 correct on the second half, the dot would be to the right of 48 on the axis for part two and directly vertical of a score of 50 for the first half (see dot in Figure 6).

The dot for student number one would be slightly to the right of the diagonal line. The greater the number of dots close to the diagonal line, the greater the inference for a reliable test.

Look at the scattergram in Figure 7 (see page 61). There appears to be a high *positive* correlation, which probably means the test has high reliability.

Look at the third scattergram (see Figure 8,

Figure 6

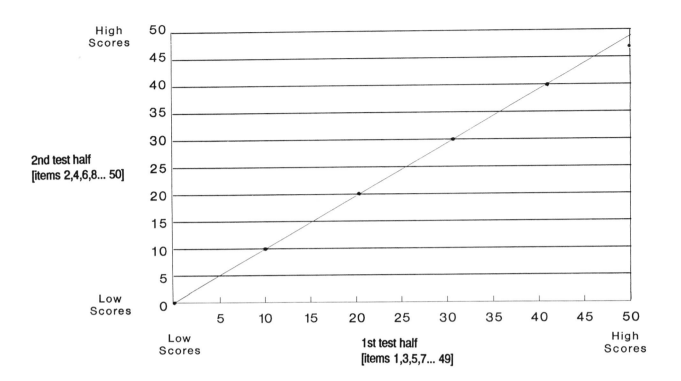

High Scores 50

45

40

35

30

25

20

15

10

5

Low Scores 0

2nd test half
[items 2,4,6,8... 50]

Low Scores   5   10   15   20   25   30   35   40   45   50   High Scores

1st test half
[items 1,3,5,7... 49]

page 62). There is a *negative* correlation, an inference that something is wrong with the reliability of the test.

Merely scanning the scattergram has been satisfactory for my own use, but other instructors may prefer the more detailed procedures of the Kuder-Richardson Formula 20, Cronbach's Coefficient Alpha, and the Pearson-Moment Coefficient of Correlation for computing the reliability of a test. These can be located in most introductory statistics books, e.g., Walter R. Borg and Meredith D. Gall, *Educational Research* (1990).

Test Administration

Another important consideration is the setting in which the students demonstrate their competencies. Environmental conditions influence performance: temperature and ventilation, seating arrangements, lighting, noise level, test materials, directions, and follow-up activities are all important.

Be sure the room is well-ventilated and at a comfortable temperature. You may need to check

the room earlier in the day to have appropriate personnel adjust the thermostat setting. Maintenance personnel can also replace burned out or flickering lights; bad fluorescent tubes drive some people crazy!

If possible, arrange the seating in such a way that the students and you feel comfortable. Students should not be crowded and should not be able to see tests others are completing.

Cheating on tests can be reduced by implementing the following suggestions:

- Revise tests periodically.

- Number all test booklets so you'll know if any are missing at the end of the test period.

- Spread out the chairs.

- Monitor the testing room.

- Use different forms of the same test with different sections of the course.

- Rearrange the order of test items for odd- and even-numbered test booklets.

There are a few other recommendations to

Figure 7

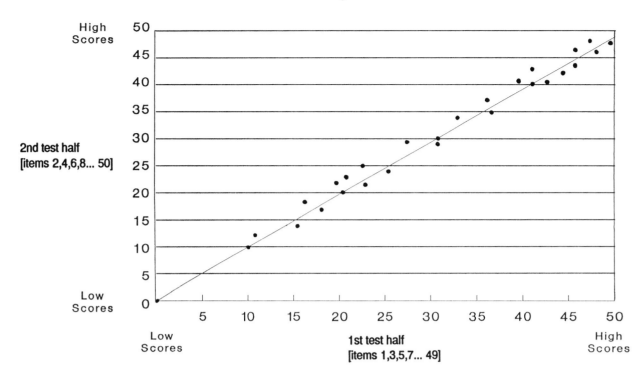

Figure 7 shows a high positive correlation, meaning the test has high reliability.

consider. Since the type of test expected by students influences their preparation, it's appropriate to tell the students in advance about the type of test. Why ask the students to "outguess" the instructor? After all, we're not evaluating extrasensory perception.

Research findings support the idea of providing space between test items so anxious students have a chance to make comments. The procedure reduces student anxiety. A student can write "This item stinks!" and then go on to obtain overall higher scores than do anxious students who have no opportunities to release their negative feelings.

Test directions should be clear. Review procedures at the beginning of the class to avoid confusion, correct typographical errors, make sure each student has all pages or materials required, answer questions, and discuss scoring procedures. Ask students to write their names on all pages in case the pages become separated. Be sensitive, straightforward, and brief. Guide, but don't hold hands or waste time.

Grading Students

Some of the most effective learning takes place after the test. Grade the test as soon as possible and discuss the results with students during the first class meeting following the grading. Discussion provides feedback and reinforces learning. It also helps you discover weaknesses in specific test items or in the test in general. Keep individual test results confidential; you don't want to embarrass students who did poorly on the test — or students who did well, by pointing them out in class. Their papers provide a suitable place for comments, questions, and compliments.

Grades are summative symbols instructors use to tell how students have performed. Judgments may be intuitive and subjective (e.g., scores assigned to essay responses), or they may be mechanical and objective (e.g., sum of all scores from a series of multiple-choice tests, rank-ordered, with the top 20% of the scores receiving an A).

Even when objective tests are used, personal biases intrude upon your "objective" judgments.

Figure 8

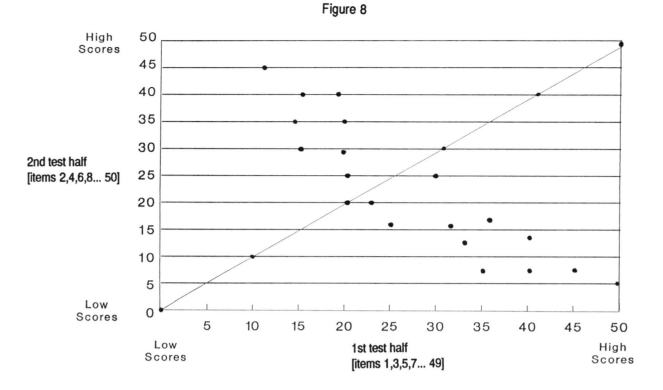

Figure 8 shows a negative correlation, meaning the test may not be reliable.

Did the multiple-choice tests represent the best basis for ranking the students? Were all items on the multiple-choice tests suitable as evidence that students accomplished the objectives for the course? Were the correct responses the only appropriate responses for the test items? Was it appropriate for only 20% of the students to receive an A?

To communicate effectively, the grading system must be simple, and yet it must deal with academic achievement. A variety of audiences must be able to understand the meaning of the grades: students, parents, administrators, employers, counselors, and personnel in other institutions, including graduate schools.

Some institutions attempt to gain uniformity among instructors by having the faculty reach a consensus about the meaning grades have in relation to a standard group of students, e.g., some may agree that a grade of A signifies that the student was in the top 15% of the group enrolled in the course, B signifies the student was in the next 25%, C signifies that the student was in the next 40%, and so forth.

One source suggests the following way of communicating the meaning of grades:

A = all major and minor objectives achieved.

A- = almost all major and minor objectives achieved.

B+ = most major and minor objectives achieved.

B = most major objectives achieved, some minor objectives not achieved.

C+ = most major objectives achieved, several minor objectives not achieved.

C = some major objectives and some minor objectives achieved, but not most of both.

D = student is not prepared for advance work.

F = failed the course.

How does an instructor or a department establish a grading system if one doesn't exist? What should one consider when establishing the system?

I would recommend that one *begin* by determining the specific purposes to be served by a grading system. The more important purposes include the following:

- To guide students.

- To help the department determine if students should continue in its program of boardsmanship. There should be a logical flow of information as we write items on the blackboard.

Answer the following questions before you write on the board:

- What do I want my students to know at the end of the lesson?

- What should I select to put on the board?

- How should I organize my statements so they have some logic and reason for being highlighted on the board?

- When should I put the materials on the board? When should I erase them?

A few more guidelines when using the board:

- Don't stand in front of your writing when lecturing. Step aside so the students can see what you are referencing when discussing items on the board.

- Don't be too quick to erase what you've written on the board. Remember: it takes students more time to logically organize and to process the information we put on the board than it takes us to fill the board with our words of wisdom. Erase only the oldest information, after you're sure the students have had ample time to copy it.

- Don't pack the board with too much information. The key is to include only *important* information. And determine in advance the "board life" of your material: some items you may need for only a few minutes, while others should remain on the board for the entire class session.

- Be the student. Walk to the back of the room and sit in the seat farthest from the board. Make sure you write or print large enough for the students to see from the back of the room. Are there any intervening obstacles, such as an overhead projector, lectern, boxes on tables, etc. that might prevent the students from seeing what's on the board?

- Write legibly; if your writing is terrible, print. Students won't benefit from our preparation if they can't interpret what we write. Be careful to write out the whole word instead of using shorthand tricks to save time. Students often write only the shortened forms — which they may no longer understand when they review their notes.

- Try to visualize the space you'll need on the board, or sketch on paper the items you want to put on the board, so you have some idea about how much space they will take. Remember that students are generally taking notes on vertical, 8 1/2" x 11" sheets of paper, while you are using a horizontal board of quite different dimensions.

- Some instructors will enter the classroom ahead of schedule and lightly outline any sketches they are going to make during a lesson. Then when they arrive at the point in the lecture when they need the sketch, they can draw heavily over the light outline or perhaps use colored chalk to highlight the sketch.

- Avoid unnecessary competition. Sometimes what you put on the board may distract students from what you're saying five minutes later.

Microcomputers

What an impact the microcomputer has had on business, government, and educational settings! It seems that today's graduates *must* know how to use microcomputers and programs because more courses are being developed that incorporate teaching through computers.

The microcomputer is transforming the world: we're using them in ever-increasing ways in business, industry, government, and our homes. There are exciting possibilities in education as well, and instructors in the '90s should make the most of our computer opportunities. Computer programs:

- Can improve study skills.

- Can "tutor" many students at their own pace through well-designed problem-solving activities.

- Can simulate experiences from the world of work.

Instructors at Texas A&M University have used incentive grants from the university's Center for Teaching Excellence to assist them in developing some very innovative microcomputer programs. They report that the time involved in developing microcomputer programs is well worth the effort.

What are the possibilities in the college setting? Here are some:

- A rule-based, computer-aided design package could assist in the design of wood structures.

- A series of interactive question-and-answer sessions could quiz students in cellular physiology and neurophysiology.

- A data base for general pathology could allow medical students to select a body part on the screen and progressively focus in on that part of the body, just as they would increase the power of a microscope.

- Self-instructional programs can provide immediate feedback and reinforcement to students in chemistry labs.

- Computerized case studies in clinical chemistry can enrich and supplement the existing curriculum.

- Testing programs, simulations, and word games can greatly enhance classroom experiences in foreign languages.

- Computer applications can be used in teaching writing and literature. Marcus, "Compupoem: A Computer-Assisted Writing Activity" (1982), provided an example of a computer program for writing poetry. Selfe, "Software for Hardness: CAI for College Composition Teachers" (1984), used a computer-assisted instruction program in first-year English composition classes. The program consisted of eight writing assignments involving description, narration, personal writing, classification, evaluation, persuasion, comparison-contrast, and literary analysis.

- Programs can be used with nursing students to develop their ability to calculate medication dosages.

- Programs can be used to implement practical experience in solving simple business problems.

- Programs can present steps in the diagnostic reasoning process, recognition of relevant and irrelevant cues, and linking cues to clinical situations for students.

- Programs can be used in physics classes to help students develop the scientific method approach in solving problems.

- Instructors in biology can use computers to teach students how to collect, retrieve, and analyze information, and then have the students draw conclusions.

An easy-to-read 1989 Phi Delta Kappa Educational Foundation Fastback also provides an excellent overview of uses of the computer with video. It may provide you with additional insight into the rapidly expanding use of computers in today's educational setting (see Beardslee and Davis, *Interactive Videodisc and the Teaching-Learning Process,* 1989).

The following are other references you may want to review:

William G. Camp, *Microcomputer Applications for Students of Agriculture,* 1988; Steven Gordon and Richard F. Anderson, *Microcomputer Applications in City Planning and Management,* 1989; Robert T. Grauer and Paul K. Sugrue, *Microcomputer Applications,* 1989; David H. Jonassen (editor), *Instructional Designs for Microcomputer Courseware,* 1988; Donald D. Spencer and Susan L. Spencer, *Drawing with a Microcomputer,* 1989; Ali Galip Ulsoy and Warren R. DeVries, *Microcomputer Applications in Manufacturing,* 1989.

study.

- To indicate to other institutions what success students might have as transfer or graduate students.
- To provide a reference point for prospective employers.

I'd encourage you to determine in advance the acceptable performance level for students in the course. I'd recommend that the performance level be directly related to your objectives established for the course. At the undergraduate level, I would recommend that an acceptable performance level always be considered a C, with the following qualifiers:

- A range of performance levels above "acceptable" exists so an ample number of students may achieve B's and A's.
- The standard curve has been rejected.
- Grades are accepted as relative, not absolute, since our reference points are not absolutely clear and dependable.

I'd also encourage the instructor to administer a typical examination on a "use or throw away basis" during the first three weeks of the course. The exam should be real, for credit, but the student should have the right to throw out this first test. Why? The first test provides early feedback to students and instructors. The "use or throw away" option provides an opportunity for the student to recover from a devastating score. A student might receive a poor grade on the first examination for various reasons: maybe he/she didn't perceive what the test would require, didn't understand what was expected, or underestimated the level of preparation needed for the examination.

By obtaining early feedback from the first examination, the student can take corrective measures and receive a final grade that would be more reflective of his/her true ability — something that wouldn't happen if the low grade were retained.

However, in the final examination for the course I believe you should include some new test items that reflect the objectives you had in mind for the first test. The students who "threw away" their first test scores must still be held accountable for accomplishing your objectives for that part of the course.

If you are interested in more in-depth coverage of testing, you might review the following references: Robert Ladd Thorndike and Elizabeth P. Hagen, *Measurement and Evaluation in Psychology and Education* (1977); Anne Anastasi, *Psychological Testing* (1988); Walter R. Borg and Meredith D. Gall, *Educational Research* (1990).

A Teaching Creed

By Glenn Ross Johnson

If you are a beginning instructor, I wish you well in your pursuit of excellence in teaching. I would like to leave you with the following *Teaching Creed* that I wrote and distributed to all faculty members, teaching assistants, and administrators at my institution when I opened the new instructional development center. Place it in a handy location so you can start your day with the *Teaching Creed* as a reminder of what you are striving to accomplish.

Although I recognize there are many different ways to teach, I believe our students are entitled to college teachers who strive to accomplish the following:

- Be well-versed in the knowledge of their subject matter.

- Be well-prepared for classes.

- Remain sincerely interested in what they teach.

- Use teaching methods which are in line with course objectives.

- Administer meaningful and well-constructed examinations.

- Remain fair and reasonable in evaluating students.

- Encourage intelligent, independent thought by students.

- Treat students with respect within and outside the classroom.

- Respond to questions to the best of their ability.

- Try to motivate students with a variety of examples and illustrations that show a practical application of content.

About the Author...

Glenn Ross Johnson is a Professor and Graduate Advisor in the College of Education at Texas A&M University. He joined the faculty at Texas A&M University in 1967 as an assistant professor of education. During his years at Texas A&M University, he has served as Head of the Department of Educational Curriculum and Instruction (1969-1974), as a Chair for the Standing Committee on Higher Education in the College of Education (1974-1985), as a Chair for the College Teaching and Research Cognate Area in the Department of Educational Curriculum and Instruction (1983-1991), and as a Director of the Texas A&M University Center for Teaching Excellence. He has authored numerous journal articles and three books in addition to First Steps to Excellence in College Teaching — A Handbook for Teaching Assistants *(1988),* Taking Teaching Seriously: A Faculty Handbook *(1988), and* Analyzing College Teaching *(1976). He twice received the "Outstanding Educator of America" award, won the "Faculty Distinguished Teaching Award" at Texas A&M University, and was a Proctor and Gamble Fellow at Columbia University, where he pursued his doctoral degree. Johnson is married and has four children and three grandchildren.*

Appendix: CIAS Practice Lesson

Directions: Cover the correct responses in the far right column with a strip of paper. Read each line, identify the category, and record your category numerals on the strip of paper. When you finish, compare your numerals with mine. If they don't match, try to figure why my numerals are different from your numerals. You may want to refer back to chapter six, where I cover the descriptions and ground rules for CIAS.

[Note: put one numeral for each hash mark (/).]

	(beginning)
	0
INSTRUCTOR:	
Let's turn our attention now to the topic/	6
of energy./ The need for energy to operate/	6 5
machinery, warm our homes, and propel our	
transportation has/ become a critical issue	5
in our country and in/ other parts of the	5
world./ Today we will discuss/ various types of	5 6
energy, including nuclear energy./ While	6
discussing this topic in class I want you/	6
to verbally identify at least four sources/	6
of energy. I also want you to verbally/	6
differentiate between fission and fusion/	6
and to identify/ at least one favorable/	6 6
aspect and one unfavorable aspect of/	6
fission and of fusion./ Excluding nuclear	6
energy, what have been our chief sources/	4
of energy?/	4
STUDENT:	
Fossil fuels./	8
INSTRUCTOR:	
Excellent, Sharon!/ And when we say fossil	2
fuels what do we have in mind primarily?/	4
STUDENT:	
Ah, coal, oil./	8
INSTRUCTOR:	
Good, Russ!/ Coal, oil—/can you think of	2 3
another?/	4
STUDENT:	
Natural gas./	8
INSTRUCTOR:	
Natural gas./ Very good, Lana!/ We do get	3 2
to a certain extent energy from another	
source./ Do you know what that source is?	5
Lana?/	4
STUDENT:	
Water power./	8
INSTRUCTOR:	
Water power,/ and in more recent years/	3 5

solar energy has emerged./ So coal, oil, | 5
natural gas, and water power have been our/ | 5
primary sources for energy to the present/ | 5
with solar energy emerging recently./ | 5
The increasing demand for fuels,/ | 5
particularly oil/ by industrialized/ | 5 5
nations, has created/ a serious problem./ | 5 5
What is that problem? Lana?/ | 4

STUDENT:
A diminishing supply./ | 8

INSTRUCTOR:
Yes, we have a diminishing supply of
fossil fuels./ Many industrialized nations/ | 3 5
are importing fuel at a great cost. If we/ | 5
can develop a different source of energy,/ | 5
particularly if it's cheap and available,/ | 5
it would be very beneficial to all/ | 5
countries. One source many are exploring is/ | 5
nuclear energy. When radioactivity was/ | 5
discovered near the end of the last century,/ | 5
physicists began to speculate about energy/ | 5
that might be stored within the atom./ In | 5
1911 they realized that the source of the/ | 4
energy was where?/ | 4

STUDENT:
In the nucleus./ | 8

INSTRUCTOR:
The nucleus./Very/good, Sharon!/ | 3 2 2
Realizing that the energy was in the
nucleus,/ their major problem until 1939 | 4
was what?/ | 4

STUDENT:
How to get the energy out of the atom./ | 8

INSTRUCTOR:
That is ... how to release the energy in a
useful way./ If we considered the measured/ | 3 5
masses of atomic nuclei we realize that/ | 5
there are two ways to make nuclear energy
available./What are those two ways?/Russ?/ | 5 4 4

STUDENT:
Fission and fusion./ | 8

INSTRUCTOR:
Fission and fusion./What is fission?/Lana?/ | 3 4 4

STUDENT:
It's the splitting apart of the atoms./ | 8

INSTRUCTOR:
Yes, splitting the heaviest nuclei into
two fairly equal parts./ Well if that's/ | 3 4
fission, what's fusion?//Russ?/ | 4 0 4

STUDENT:
Bringing together of two nuclei./ | 8

INSTRUCTOR:

The combining of the lighter nuclei./	3
The appeal of fission and fusion will be/	4
what? Lana?/	4

STUDENT:

It's self-sustaining .../it keeps on going./	8 8

INSTRUCTOR:

Very good./ Once started it has the	2
possibility of becoming/ self sustaining and	3
producing more energy than/ is consumed and	3
causing the reaction to occur./ When nuclear	3
fission was discovered in 1939, it uncovered/	5
a highly concentrated energy source; and,/	5
we know the history of the development of/	5
the atomic bomb and nuclear reactors. The/	5
availability of uranium is presently/	5
appealing, but fission may not be the/	5
complete solution to the energy problem./	5
Why?/ Russ?/	4 4

STUDENT:

Well, we're running out of uranium, too./	8

INSTRUCTOR:

Eventually we'll probably run into a/	3
diminishing supply of uranium/ plus some	3
countries do not have access to uranium./	5
So we now turn to nuclear fusion/ as a	6
possible power source./ What is the/	6 4
essential fuel material for fusion?/ Lana?/	4 4

STUDENT:

Hydrogen./	8

INSTRUCTOR:

A form of hydrogen./ Do you know what we	3
call that heavy hydrogen?/	4

STUDENT:

Deuterium./	8

INSTRUCTOR:

That's right, deuterium./ Why is this	3
appealing?/ Lana?/	4 4

STUDENT:

Because it's available from water./	8

INSTRUCTOR:

Yes, and we have a lot of water./ It has	3
been theoretically calculated that the/	5
energy potential from the deuterium nuclei/	5
present in a gallon of water is equal to/	5
the combustion of 300 gallons of/	5
gasoline./ Is it costly to extract deuterium/	5 4
in a gallon of water?/ Russ?/	4 4

STUDENT:

No, it's not./	8

INSTRUCTOR:

No, it's not./ It's cheap, a few pennies/   3 5
per gallon of water./ So the fuel source is   5
cheap, it's abundant,/ it's available.   5
Unfortunately,/ there are several problems/   5 5
about fusion power./ Can nuclear fusion even/   4
be achieved?/ Russ?/   4 4

STUDENT:
Yes./   8

INSTRUCTOR:
Yes./ We have been able to do it   3
experimentally./ Laboratories have   5
accelerated deuterium/ nuclei to a high   5
velocity in cyclotrons, and/ when they hit   5
a solid target containing deuterium,/ fusion   5
reactions take place,/ but most of the   5
energy is dissipated as heat/ in the target   5
because only a small/ number of accelerated   5
deuterium nuclei collide with those on/   5
the target, thus we spend more energy than
we produce./ It is the search for more ways/   5 6
to generate more energy/ than we spend/   6 6
that we will deal with theoretically during/   6
the next few weeks when we continue our
discussion/ of nuclear fusion./ To summarize,   6 6
we have identified coal,/ oil, natural gas,/ and   6 5
water power as our chief sources of energy,/   5
with solar energy coming into the picture/   5
in recent years. We differentiated between/   5
fission, the splitting of the heaviest/   5
nuclei into two equal parts, and fusion,/   5
combination of the lightest nuclei. The/   5
availability of uranium and the ability to/   5
split the nuclei/ is a strength for fission./   5 5
A limitation is its unavailability to all/   5
nations and eventually a problem with/   5
supply. The appeal of fusion is that it/   5
uses a form of hydrogen, deuterium,/   5
available to everyone in water. The major/   5
limitation is the inability to combine the/   5
lightest nuclei/ without expending more/   5 5
energy than we can produce./ We'll continue   5
with this/ topic next class session./   6 6
    0
(end of transcript)

Bibliography

Anastasi, Anne (1988). *Psychological Testing,* sixth edition. New York: Macmillan.

Ball, Samuel (Ed.) (1977). *Motivation in Education.* New York: Academic Press.

Barratt, Leslie (1988). "Ten Things That Teachers Should Teach (and Students Should Learn) About Language." *Contemporary Education, 59* (2), 70-71.

Barrow, Gordon M. (1980). Computer-Based Studies for Physical Chemistry. *Journal of Chemical Education, 57,* 697-702.

Beardslee, Edward C., and Geoffrey L. Davis (1989). *Interactive Videodisc and the Teaching-Learning Process.* Bloomington IN: Phi Delta Kappa Educational Foundation.

Behr, A.L. (1988). "Exploring the Lecture Method: An Empirical Study." *Studies in Higher Education, 13* (2), 189-200.

Benjamin, Moshe, Wilbert J. McKeachie, Yi-Guang Lin, and Dorothy P. Holinger (1981). "Test Anxiety: Deficits in Information Processing." *Journal of Educational Psychology, 73* (6), 816-824.

Bennett, William J. (1984). *To Reclaim a Legacy: A Report on the Humanities in Higher Education.* Washington: National Endowment for the Humanities.

Bergan, John R., and James A. Dunn (1976). *Psychology and Education: A Science for Instruction.* New York: John Wiley and Sons.

Bloom, Benjamin S. (1976). *Human Characteristics and School Learning.* New York: McGraw-Hill.

Bloom, Benjamin S. (Ed.) (1956). *Taxonomy of Educational Objectives.* New York: David McKay.

Bloom, Benjamin S., J. Thomas Hastings, and George F. Madaus (1971). *Handbook on Formative and Summative Evaluation of Student Learning.* New York: McGraw-Hill.

Bok, Derek (1986). *Higher Learning.* Cambridge: Harvard University Press.

Bok, Derek (1986). *President's Report to the Board of Overseers.* Unpublished manuscript. Cambridge: Harvard University.

Borg, Walter R., and Meredith D. Gall (1990). *Educational Research,* fifth edition. New York: Longman.

Boyer, Ernest L. (1987). *College: The Undergraduate Experience in America.* New York: Harper and Row.

Brookfield, Stephen D. (1987). *Developing Critical Thinkers: Challenging Adults to Explore Alternative Ways of Thinking and Acting.* San Francisco: Jossey-Bass.

Brown, George B., and Madeleine Atkins (1988). *Effective Teaching.* London: Methuen.

Brown, James W., and James Thornton, Jr. (1971). *College Teaching: A Systematic Approach,* second edition. New York: McGraw-Hill.

Browne, M. Neil, and Stuart M. Keeley (1988). "Do College Students Know How to 'Think Critically' When They Graduate?" *Research Serving Teaching,* a newsletter published by the Southwest Missouri State University Center for Teaching and Learning, 1 (9), 1-2.

Bugelski, Bergen R. (1971). *The Psychology of Learning Applied to Teaching.* New York: Bobbs-Merrill.

Bullard, John R., and Calvin E. Mether (1984). *Audiovisual Fundamentals: Basic Equipment Operation, Simple Materials Production,* third edition. Dubuque IA: W.C. Brown.

Camp, William G. (1988). *Microcomputer Applications for Students of Agriculture.* Danville IL: Interstate Printers & Publishers.

Carl, L.M. (1982). "PR and Creativity." *Journalism Education, 37* (1:Spring), 6-8.

Carroll, John B. (1989). "The Carroll Model: A 25-Year Retrospective and Prospective View." *Educational Researcher, 18* (1), 26-31.

Cavin, Claudia S., E.D. Cavin, and J.J. Lagowski (1980). "The Use of Microcomputers in College Teaching." *Educational Technology, 20,* 41-43.

Chickering, Arthur W., and Zelda F. Gamson (1987). "Seven Principles for Good Practice in Undergraduate Education." *AAHE Bulletin, 39* (7), 3-7.

Christensen, C. Roland, and Abby J. Hansen (1987). *Teaching and the Case Method.* Boston: Harvard Business School.

Clarke, John H. (1987). "Building a Lecture That Really Works." *The Education Digest* (October), 52-55.

Colorado, Rafael J. (1988). "Computer-Assisted Instruction Research: A Critical Assessment." *Journal of Research on Computing in Education, 20*, 226-233.

Cross, Patricia K. (1986). "A Proposal to Improve Teaching, or What 'Taking Teaching Seriously' Should Mean." *AAHE Bulletin, 39* (1), 9-15.

Cross, K. Patricia, and Thomas A. Angelo (1988). *Classroom Assessment Techniques: A Handbook for Faculty.* Ann Arbor MI: National Center for the Improvement of Postsecondary Teaching and Learning.

Crovello, Theodore J. (1982). "Computers in Biological Education." *American Biology Teacher, 44*, 76-83.

Diamond, Nancy A., M. Helgesen, and P. Visek (undated). *Teaching Large Classes.* Illini Instructor Series, No. 1. Office of Instructional and Management Services. Urbana-Champaign: University of Illinois.

Eble, Kenneth E. (1976). *The Craft of Teaching: A Guide to Mastering the Professor's Art.* San Francisco: Jossey-Bass.

Engh, Steve, and Kenneth L. Ratzlaff (1980). "The Use of Computer-Assisted Instruction in the Teaching Laboratory." *Journal of Chemical Education, 57*, 815-818.

Essex, D.L., and W.E. Sorlie (1979). "Effectiveness of Instructional Computers in Teaching Basic Medical Sciences." *Medical Education, 13*, 189-193.

Flanders, Ned A. (1970). *Analyzing Teaching Behavior.* Reading MA: Addison-Wesley.

Flanders, Ned A. (1965). *Teacher Influence, Pupil Attitudes, and Achievement.* Cooperative Research Monograph No. 12, U.S. Office of Education. Washington: U.S. Government Printing Office.

Frederick, Peter J. (1986). "The Lively Lecture — 8 Variations." *College Teaching, 34* (2:Spring), 43-50.

Fuhrmann, Barbara S., and Anthony F. Grasha (1983). *A Practical Handbook for College Teachers.* Boston: Little, Brown & Co.

Gadzella, Bernadette M. (1982). "Computer-Assisted Instruction and Study Skills." *Journal of Experimental Education, 50*, 122-128.

Galbraith, Michael W., and Ray E. Sanders (1987). "Relationship Between Perceived Learning Style and Teaching Style of Junior College Educators." *Community/Junior College Quarterly of Research and Practice,* 11, 169-177.

Gall, Meredith D., and Joyce P. Gall (1976). "The Discussion Method." *The Psychology of Teaching Methods.* Seventy-Fifth Yearbook of the National Society for the Study of Education, Part I, pp. 166-216. Chicago: University of Chicago Press.

Gleason, Maryellen (1986). "An Instructor Survival Kit for Use with Large Classes." *AAHE Bulletin, 39* (2:October), 10-14.

Gifford, Vernon D., and Joann Vick (1982). "A Comparison of the Personalized System of Instruction and a Conventional Biology Course on the Achievement of Junior College Freshmen." *Journal of Research in Science Teaching, 19* (8), 659-664.

Gordon, Steven I., and Richard F. Anderson (1989). *Microcomputer Applications in City Planning and Management.* New York: Praeger.

Grauer, Robert T., and Paul K. Sugrue (1989). *Microcomputer Applications,* second edition. New York: McGraw-Hill.

Hansen, Abby J. (1987). "Suggestions for Seminar Participants." In C. Roland Christensen, *Teaching and the Case Method,* 54-59. Boston: Harvard Business School.

Hess, C.W. (1988). "Thinking about Thinking: Bloom's Taxonomy Rediscovered." *Faculty Development,* a regional, collaborative newsletter for Bush-funded programs in Minnesota, North Dakota, and South Dakota, *1* (3), 2-3.

Hliva, W.R., D.M. Holden, and R.L. Klick (1982). "Computerized Instructional Case Studies in Clinical Chemistry." *Laboratory Medicine, 13*, 246-251.

Hunt, Pearson (1951). "The Case Method of Instruction." *Harvard Educational Review, 21* (3:Summer), 175-192.

Integrity in the College Community: A Report to the Academic Community (1985). Washington:

Association of American Colleges.

Involvement in Learning: Realizing the Potential of American Higher Education (1984). National Institute of Education, Study Group on the Conditions of Excellence in American Higher Education. Washington: U.S. Government Printing Office.

Johnson, Glenn Ross (1975). *Improving College Teaching via Microteaching and Interaction Analysis: A Handbook for Professors and Prospective Instructors.* Abstract ERIC Documents ED 102-933, ED 102-286, 105-067, IR 001-429. Vol. 10.

Johnson, Glenn Ross (1975). *Enhancing College Teaching.* ERIC Document Reproduction Service ED 118-044, ED 118.

Johnson, Glenn Ross (1976). *Analyzing College Teaching.* Manchaca TX: Sterling Swift Publishing.

Johnson, Glenn Ross (1976). "Delphi-Process Evaluation of the Effectiveness of Selected In-Service Training Techniques to Improve Community/Junior College Instruction." *Community/Junior College Research Quarterly, 1* (1), 51-57.

Johnson, Glenn Ross (1987). "An Eclectic Systematic Instruction Model for Expository Instruction." *Journal of Staff, Program and Organization Development, 5* (3), 91-99.

Johnson, Glenn Ross (1987). "Changing the Verbal Behavior of Teachers." *Journal of Staff, Program and Organization Development, 5* (4), 155-158.

Johnson, Glenn Ross, James A. Eison, Robert Abbott, Guy T. Meiss, Kathy Moran, Joyce A. Morgan, Thomas L. Pasternack, Ernest Zaremba, and Wilbert J. McKeachie (1991). *Teaching Tips for Users of the Motivated Strategies for Learning Questionnaire (MSLQ).* Ann Arbor MI: National Center for Research to Improve Postsecondary Teaching and Learning.

Jonassen, David H. (1988). *Instructional Designs for Microcomputer Courseware.* Hillsdale NJ: L. Erlbaum Associates.

Kagan, Dona M. (1987). "Stress in the College and University Classroom: A Synthesis of Eight Empirical Studies." *College Student Journal, 21* (4), 312-316.

Kaiser, B. (1988). "Cooperative Learning Revisited." *Faculty Development, 1* (2), 2-3.

Korobkin, Debra (1988). "Humor in the Classroom: Considerations and Strategies." *College Teaching, 36* (4), 154-158).

Kulik, James A., C. Chen-Lin, and P.A. Cohen (1979). "Research on Audio-Tutorial Instruction: A Meta-Analysis of Comparative Studies." *Research in Higher Education, 11* (4), 321-341.

Kushner, J. (1983). "Computer-Assisted Instruction in Hematology." *Laboratory Medicine, 14,* 307-309.

Lefrancois, Guy R. (1972). *Psychological Theories and Human Learning: Kongor's Report.* Monterey CA: Brooks/Cole Publishing.

Learned, Edmund P. (1987). "Reflections of a Case Method Teacher." In C. Roland Christensen, *Teaching and the Case Method,* 9-15. Boston: Harvard Business School.

Lewis, R., and J. Harris (1980). "Physics Education With or Without Computers." *Computers and Education, 4* (1), 11-14.

Locatis, Craig N., and Francis D. Atkinson (1984). *Media and Technology for Education and Training.* Columbus OH: Charles E. Merrill Publishing.

Lower, Stephan K. (1981). "An Audio-Tutorial Approach to the Teaching of Physical Chemistry and Electrochemistry." *Journal of Chemical Education, 58* (19), 773-776.

Marcus, Stephen (1982). "Compupoem: A Computer-Assisted Writing Activity." *English Journal, 71* (2), 96-99.

McLeish, John (1976). "The Lecture Method." In *The Psychology of Teaching Methods.* Seventy-Fifth Yearbook of the National Society for the Study of Education, Part I. Chicago: University of Chicago Press.

McKeachie, Wilbert J. (1986). *Teaching Tips: A Guidebook for the Beginning College Teacher.* Lexington MA: D.C. Heath.

Mickler, M.L., and C.P. Zippert (1987). "Teaching Strategies Based on Learning." *Community/Junior College Quarterly, 11* (1), 33-37.

Miles, L., and Harold W. Stubblefield (1982). "Learning Groups in Training and Education." *Small Group Behavior, 13* (3:August), 311-320.

Morris, Larry W., Mark A. Davis, and Calvin H. Hutchings (1981). "Cognitive and Emotional Components of Anxiety: Literature Review and a Revised Worry-Emotional Scale." *Journal of Educational*

Psychology, 73, 541-555.

Mott, Charles J. (1980). "Ten Years of Experimentation in Audio-Tutorial Systems." *Journal of Geological Education, 28* (5:November), 233-234.

Newman, Frank (1987). "The Growth of State Mandates Aimed at Improving Quality." In Frank Newman, *Choosing Quality: Reducing Conflict Between the State and the University.* Denver: Education Commission of the States.

Pintrich, Paul R., David A.F. Smith, Teresa Garcia, and Wilbert J. McKeachie (1991). *A Manual for the Use of the Motivated Strategies for Learning Questionnaire (MSLQ).* Ann Arbor MI: National Center for Research to Improve Postsecondary Teaching and Learning.

Postlethwait, Samuel N., J. Novak, H.T. Murray, Jr. (1969). *The Audio-Tutorial Approach to Learning: Through Independent Study and Integrated Experiences,* second edition. Minneapolis: Burgess.

Powell, J.P., and L.W. Andresen (1985). "Humor and Teaching in Higher Education." *Studies in Higher Education, 10* (1), 79-90.

Powers, Donald E., and Mary K. Enright (1987). "Analytical Reasoning Skills in Graduate Study." *Journal of Higher Education, 58* (6), 658-682.

"Practical Poetry: Metaphoric Thinking in Science, Art, Literature and Nearly Everywhere Else (1987). *Teaching-Learning Issues, 60* (Fall). Learning Research Center, University of Tennessee.

Pusack, James P. (1981). "Computer-Assisted Instruction in Foreign Language." *Pipeline, 10,* 5-8.

Ramsden, Paul (1987). "Improving Teaching and Learning in Higher Education: The Case for a Relational Perspective." *Studies in Higher Education, 12* (3), 275-286.

Reynold, A., and S. Pontious (1986). "CAI Enhances the Medication Dosage Calculation Competency of Nursing Students." *Computers in Nursing, 4* (4:July/August), 158-165.

Rosenshine, Barak (1976). "Classroom Instruction." *The Psychology of Teaching Methods.* Seventy-Fifth Yearbook of the National Society for the Study of Education, part I, 335-371. Chicago: University of Chicago Press.

Sappington, A.A., and W. E. Farrar (1982). "Critical Judgment in the Generation of Solutions Which Conform to Reality Constraints." *The Journal of Creative Behavior, 16* (1), 68-73.

Schlenker, Richard M. and Constance M. Perry (1986). "Planning Lectures that Start, Go, and End Somewhere." *Journal of College Science Teaching, 15* (5:March/April), 440-442.

Schwartz, Helen J. (1982). "Monsters and Mentors: Computer Applications for Humanistic Education." *College English,* 141-152.

Self, Samuel (1973). *Flanders' Interaction Analysis and a Token Economy in College Physics Instruction.* Unpublished doctoral dissertation, Texas A&M University, College Station.

Selfe, Cynthia L. (1984). "Software for Hardness: CAI for College Composition Teachers." *Educational Technology, 24* (8:September), 25-29.

Shavelson, Richard J. (1976). "Teachers' Decision-Making." *The Psychology of Teaching.* Seventy-Fifth Yearbook of the National Society for the Study of Education, Part I, 372-414. Chicago: University of Chicago Press.

Smith, B. Othanel (1971). *Research in Teacher Education: A Symposium.* Englewood Cliffs NJ: Prentice-Hall.

Smith, Herman W. (1987). "Comparative Evaluation of Three Teaching Methods of Quantitative Techniques: Traditional Lecture, Socratic Dialogue, and PSI Format." *Journal of Experimental Education, 55* (3), 149-154.

Spencer, Donald D., and Susan L. Spencer (1989). *Drawing with a Microcomputer.* Ormond Beach FL: Camelot Publishing Company.

Staats, W.L. (1982). "A Computer Programming Course for Accountants, Business Practitioners, and College Students." *Computers and Education, 6,* 193-198.

Sternberg, Robert J. (1985). "Teaching Critical Thinking, Part I: Are We Making Critical Mistakes?" *Phi Delta Kappan, 67* (3), 194-198.

Symonds, Percival M. (1968). *What Education Has to Learn From Psychology,* third edition. New York: Teachers College Press.

Thiele, Joan E., Joan H. Baldwin, Robert S. Hyde, Beth Sloan, and Gloria A. Strandquist (1986). "An Investigation of Decision Theory: What Are the Effects of Teaching Cue Recognition?" *Journal of Nursing Education, 25* (8:October), 319-324.

Thorndike, Robert Ladd, and Elizabeth P. Hagen (1977). *Measurement and Evaluation in Psychology and Education,* fourth edition. New York: Wiley.

Todd, William D. (1982). "Brainstorming." *Industrial Education, 71* (2:February), 22-23.

Tubb, Gary (1974). *Heuristic Questioning and Problem-Solving Strategies in Mathematics Graduate Teaching Assistants and Their Students.* Unpublished doctoral dissertation, Texas A&M University, College Station.

Ulsoy, Ali Galip, and Warren R. DeVries (1989). *Microcomputer Applications in Manufacturing.* New York: Wiley.

Vietor, Donald M., S.C. Brubaker, Murray H. Milford, and Glenn Ross Johnson (1985). "Teacher Improvement Using a Cognitive Interaction Analysis System." *Journal of Agronomic Education, 14* (1), 44-48.

Wagner, J. (Ed.) (1983). "Large Classes and Beginning Students." *Teaching at Berkeley, 6* (1:Spring), 2-3. University of California, Berkeley.

Watson, Jane M. (1986). "The Keller Plan, Final Examinations, and Long-Term Retention." *Journal for Research in Mathematics Education, 17* (1), 60-68.

Weaver II, Richard L., and Howard W. Cottrell (1988). "Motivating Students: Stimulating and Sustaining Student Effort." *College Student Journal, 22* (1), 22-32.

Wharton, Clifton R., Jr. (1987). "Taking Teachers Seriously." *AAHE Bulletin, 39* (9 & 10), 7-11.

Whipple, William R. (1987). "Collaborative Learning: Recognizing It When We See It." *AAHE Bulletin, 40* (2), 3-6.

Wiegers, Karl E., and S.G. Smith (1980). "The Use of Computer-Based Chemistry Lessons in the Organic Laboratory Course." *Journal of Chemical Education, 57,* 454-456.

Williams, David D. (1985). "University Class Size: Is Smaller Better?" *Research in Higher Education, 23* (3), 307-317.

Wittrock, Merlin C. (Ed.) (1977). *Learning and Instruction.* Berkeley: McCutchan Publishing.

Wright, Delivee L. (1987). "Selecting the Textbook." *Teaching at UNL.* Lincoln: University of Nebraska-Lincoln.

Wulff, Donald H., and Jody D. Nyquist (1988). "Using Field Methods as an Instructional Tool." *To Improve the Academy,* 87-98. Stillwater OK: New Forums Press.

OTHER TITLES FOR HIGHER EDUCATION FACULTY
AND ACADEMIC ADMINISTRATORS

Mentor in a Manual: Climbing the Academic Ladder to Tenure (Product #51BP)
Most faculty will find this book most helpful, covering all the important tenure areas with valuable advice from years of experience. A special Appendix – What Do I Do if I Don't Make Tenure? — may be as valuable to some as the manual itself. Price: $29.95.

Classroom Communication: Collected Readings for Effective Discussion and Questioning (Product #16BP)
The editors have assembled articles that effectively address current problems and practices in the classroom. This collection of readings is written to accommodate even the busiest instructor. Price: $22.50.

Teaching College: Collected Readings for the New Instructor (Product #18BP)
Designed for teaching assistants and part-time instructors with little or no college teaching experience, this collection of readings contains ideas, information, and advice about issues confronting new teachers as they undertake instructional responsibility for the first time. Price: $21.95.

147 Practical Tips for Teaching Professors (Product #25BP)
This handbook serves as a useful guide for teachers who look to improve their performance in the classroom. Included are tips, techniques hints, and suggestions for teachers – from teachers. Price: $12.50.

How Am I Teaching? Forms and Activities for Acquiring Instructional Input (Product #26BP)
This workbook serves as an excellent source of new ideas for improving instructional effectiveness. If you are looking for better ways to improve instructional quality, use **How Am I Teaching?** as a means for instructors to collect valuable information. Price: $24.95.